ROUTLEDGE LIBRARY EDITIONS: CHINESE LITERATURE AND ARTS

Volume 10

CONTEMPORARY CHINESE POETRY

CONTEMPORARY CHINESE POETRY

Edited by
ROBERT PAYNE

LONDON AND NEW YORK

First published in 1947 by George Routledge & Sons Ltd.

This edition first published in 2022
by Routledge
4 Park Square, Milton Park, Abingdon, Oxon OX14 4RN

and by Routledge
605 Third Avenue, New York, NY 10158

Routledge is an imprint of the Taylor & Francis Group, an informa business

© 1947

All rights reserved. No part of this book may be reprinted or reproduced or utilised in any form or by any electronic, mechanical, or other means, now known or hereafter invented, including photocopying and recording, or in any information storage or retrieval system, without permission in writing from the publishers.

Trademark notice: Product or corporate names may be trademarks or registered trademarks, and are used only for identification and explanation without intent to infringe.

British Library Cataloguing in Publication Data
A catalogue record for this book is available from the British Library

ISBN: 978-0-367-11183-0 (Set)
ISBN: 978-1-032-24546-1 (Volume 10) (hbk)
ISBN: 978-1-032-24547-8 (Volume 10) (pbk)
ISBN: 978-1-003-27920-4 (Volume 10) (ebk)

DOI: 10.4324/9781003279204

Publisher's Note
The publisher has gone to great lengths to ensure the quality of this reprint but points out that some imperfections in the original copies may be apparent.

Disclaimer
The publisher has made every effort to trace copyright holders and would welcome correspondence from those they have been unable to trace.

EDITED WITH AN INTRODUCTION BY
ROBERT PAYNE

CONTEMPORARY CHINESE POETRY

ROUTLEDGE · LONDON

First published in England
by GEORGE ROUTLEDGE & SONS LTD.
Broadway House, 68-74 Carter Lane,
London, E.C.4
1947

Printed in Great Britain
at The Westminster Press
411a Harrow Road
London, W.9

CONTENTS

PREFACE	*page* ix
INTRODUCTION	xi

HSU CHIH-MO

translated by Yuan K'o-chia	35
Farewell to Cambridge	37
A Song of the Sea	38
Follow Me	39
The Snow	40
Love	41
The Beggar	42
Listening to the Bells	43
One Night at Florence	44

WEN YI-TUO

translated by Ho Yung	47
A Vassal	49
Autumn Beauty	49
Dead Water	52
Perhaps	53
Chess-player	54
The Confession	54
The Last Day	54
I Come, I Shout . . .	55
The Stream	55
The Heart Beats	56
Early Summer Night	57

Death	*page* 57
Spring Rain	58
The Deserted Village	59

Ho Chih-Fang

translated by Chiang Shao-yi	63
The Stream	64
O Storm, O Thunder	64
The Things that Remain	65
The Fable	65
Let Me Speak of Pure Things	66
Night Song I	67
Night Song II	68
Happiness	70

Feng Chih

translated by Chu K'an	71
Fifteen Sonnets	72

Pien Chih-Lin

translated by Pien Chih-lin	81
Peking	83
The Composition of Distances	85
The Aqueous Rock	85
Fragment	86
First Lamp	86
Resounding Dust	86
Solitude	87
Fish Fossil	87
Late on a Festival Night	87
The Rain and I	88
Tears	88
The Migration of Birds	89
The Peninsula	90

The History of Communications	page 90
The Doormat and the Blotting Paper	90
The Girl at the Dressing Table	90
Notes to Pien Chih-lin's Poems	92

YU MIN-CHUAN

translated by Yu Min-chuan	97
Lady Macbeth	99
Waking at the Dead Hour	99
With a Precious Stone	100
The Night-Raiding Plane	100
High the Sky	101
Rustling	102
Horses	102
Why?	103
The Auction	104
The Child	105
The Two Eyes	106

TSENG K'O-CHIA

translated by Chang Tao	107
The Sea	108
The Nameless Star	108
Silence	109
The Dead Water	110
Stillness	110
Tears, Sweat, and Pearls	111
Midday Rest	111
A Grave	112
The Farm	113
The Return	113
Ricksha-Driver	114
There will Soon be a Day	114

AI CHING

    translated by Ho Chih-yuan   *page* 117
    The Man Who Died a Second Time   119
    Snow Falls in China   130
    The Winter Forest   133
    Desolation   134
    The Land Revived   134
    The Words of the Sun   135
    Invocation to the Dawn   136
    North China   137

TIEN CHIEN

    translated by Chu Chun-I   141
    In the Morning We are Training   143
    One Gun, One Chang-I   143
    The Black Horse, the Pistol and the Song   146
    Freedom is Coming Towards Us   146
    I have only a Draft of Paper and some Stains of Blood   147
    The Land is Laughing for You   147
    Song of the Mountains   148
    We are Forever Young   148
    More than One Hundred   149
    Down with the Enemy   150
    The People's Dance   150
    She, too, wants to Kill a Man   155

APPENDIX: The Drummer of the Age   165

PREFACE

SINCE *the publication of Mr. Harold Acton's excellent volume of* Modern Chinese Poetry *in 1936, no comprehensive anthology of modern Chinese poetry has appeared in English. I had thought at one time of making an anthology of poems produced since the Lukouchiao incident and the beginning of the war against Japan, but it seemed better to retrace some of the ground covered by the previous volume to show the development from the Chinese Renaissance Movement to the present time—the time of Tien Chien and Ai Ching, with their extraordinary power and their continual poetic innovations. With these two poets, and with many of the later poets included in this book, Chinese poetry enters at last into an entirely new world, where all, or nearly all, of the ancient poetic traditions are cast aside: and those who still think of Chinese poetry as the graceful accomplishment of retired sages may do well to ponder the brutality, power and honesty of the new poetry which is being produced to-day.*

I have to thank Mr. Pien Chih-lin and Mr. Yu Min-chuan for their translations of their own poems, and Dr. Wen Yi-tuo and Dr. Feng Chih for their careful revisions of the translations of their poems made by others. I have to thank the translators of the remaining poems not only for their translations, but for their kindness during the endless discussions which led to the making of this book.

IN MEMORIAM
WEN YI-TUO

INTRODUCTION

I

IN the year 1926 there gathered in Peking a group of young poets who were determined to change the direction in which Chinese poetry was going. China was at peace. The northward march of the Kuomintang Army was still little more than a madcap paper scheme to dominate the country by force of arms, and in the long Peking summer there was an air of peace, and even of splendour, for men were beginning to think that the long years of civil war would soon come to an end. Among these poets there was Hsu Chih-mo, who had recently left Nanking and taken up a professorship at Peking University: there was Chu Hsiung, Liu Meng-wei and Wen Yi-tuo. All were to become famous in different ways; none were to survive. Hsu Chih-mo was killed in an air-crash at Tsinanfu, not far from the holy mountain of T'ai Shan; Chiu Hsiung drowned himself in the Yangtse; Liu Meng-wei burnt himself out at an early age, having shown even in his youth a promise which was sometimes blinded by the achievements of others; Wen Yi-tuo, the greatest of all, was assassinated by soldiers. It was the first time in the history of modern China that so many prominent poets had come together to discuss the foundations of poetry, for the revival of *pai hua* by Dr. Hu Shih in his famous essay of 1917 had done no more than indicate the path to be travelled, and no great poetry had arisen to justify the theories of the innovators. According to the literary critic Liang Shih-chiu, the meeting was frought with heavy consequences. "They insisted on the importance of form, they tried to invent new forms and they made better use of the old ones. Their greatest achievement was in constructing a solid foundation for poetry, and they were the first to re-introduce a conception of pure form, which had vanished as soon as the heavy restraints of the past had been lifted. We were even beginning to doubt the possibility of any new poetry at all; and it is to Wen Yi-tuo above all that we must credit the introduction of a conception of poetry, and of a technique of poetry, which is modelled on the other arts. Wen Yi-tuo claimed that poetry should possess at once the beauty of music, of painting and of architecture. The beauty of music implies rhythm and rhyme, the beauty of painting implies colour and rhetoric and the beauty of architecture implies form and structure". With these meetings the wheel turned full circle. There was no longer a guarded hatred of form; and the experimenters began, at first slowly but later with increasing power and speed, to reintroduce the old Chinese forms and to explore the forms used in the West.

This revolution, however, did not owe everything to Wen Yi-tuo, even though Hsu Chih-mo was to say later: "We are all of us in a certain measure influenced by the author of the *Dead Water*." It owed, perhaps, most to the spirit of the times, and to the accident that the great majority of the better poets were educated abroad. Those who retained their feeling for form longest were usually those who had been educated in England, France and America; those who secretly fought against form were the returned students from Japan, the anarchists, the young poets whose impulses refused to be bound within the limits of a form, however necessary. But form remained. It was a dangerous element in those years when China was at last awakening from a deep sleep; but it was necessary at its time in spite of the inherent dangers which it brought into poetry. The poets were rarely able to master the forms. The introduction of western forms on a language which possesses an infinity of rhymes and a vocabulary where nearly every word has precisely two syllables could not always be successful. Liang Tsong-tai experimented with the sonnet, which Feng Chih was to employ later, and, though he failed to write great poetry, his achievements as a translator of Valéry placed him in the enviable position of being for a while the most outstanding mediator between the Boulevard St. Michel and Peking. The sonnet is now an accepted form in Chinese poetry: so, too, is the poem which consists of an unknown number of quatrains, though these had already existed in the Chinese ballad. The earliest influences on Chinese poetry after the revolutions of 1911 were all English. It was Dr. Hu Shih's regard for Browning, and Hsu Chih-mo's passion for Keats and Wordsworth which brought about the new beginnings. And Hsu Chih-mo himself, with his Byronic beauty, his flair for modernity, his charm and his delicacy, who crystallised in an almost perfect manner the aspirations of the young poets of his time, became the inevitable leader, and afterwards the inevitable scapegoat for the movement which was still too little rooted on the soil of China. There is a sentimentality in the poems of the renaissance which is surprising in men so talented, a sentimentality which is excusable in the poetry of Ping Hsing (who was after all only a woman) but inexcusable in an undergraduate of King's College, Cambridge. To the last Hsu Chih-mo retained a flair for the most terrible sentimental inversions, and it is only necessary to compare his poem *The Beggar* with Tseng K'o-chia's *Ricksha-driver*, a far inferior poem, to realise how far Hsu Chih-mo remained from the world of men even when he had most pity for them. The sentimentality which had been the curse of the Ming and Ch'ing Dynasties tormented the revolutionary successors of the imperial splendour. With the death of Hsu Chih-mo, a small era in Chinese poetry came to an end. Form as an end in itself, or even as something to be acquired by the sweat of one's brow, was seen to be less important than the menacing approach over the northern barriers of the Japanese.

Wen Yi-tuo had shown surprising powers of survival. He possessed a toughness which was lacking in his predecessors, and a gift for savage irony which would have been tormenting if he had failed to possess an essential purity of soul. He returned from America with no desire to continue painting, but with an unappeasable thirst for the old culture of China. He read widely. He taught himself to be entirely independent in his interpretations of the ancient classics, and though for a period he seems to have been obsessed with Confucian virtues, they vanished quickly enough as he contemplated the civil wars. He was a revolutionary from the beginning, but before there was any beginning at all he must have been a scholar. It was the scholar's temperament which cried out for form; it was the scholar's bitterness and irony which shaped the *Red Candles* and *The Dead Water*. He could not sing like Hsu Chih-mo and his friend Chu-Hsiung was to say of him that "though he wrote elaborately and carefully, no one ever heard him sing naturally" Wen Yi-tuo could have answered there was nothing to sing about—only the interminable disgraces of poverty and civil wars. He said nothing. He was far too engrossed in his interpretations of the classics.

There is a sense in which it is true that Wen Yi-tuo is the greatest and also the least of modern Chinese poets. He had founded a movement, written within the laws he had evolved from the silence of a rooming-house in Chicago, launched his two small collections of poetry on the world and in the desperate years following the invasion of Manchuria he turned his back on poetry and retreated into the world of scholarship, where the forms are even more exigent than in poetry. But perhaps there was no other way. There is a ghostly savagery in some of his poems which suggests that the poet had come to the edge of madness, and even in such a short fragment as:

> In the silent tides of evening
> Always there comes stealing into my desolate braid
> Queer whims, inconceivable and strange,
> As from a dusky, dank belfry before an ancient temple
> There flies out a flock of frightened bats,
> That non-animal, non-bird thing, the devil. . . .

we feel the weight of the hidden desolation, and it is not difficult to relate it to the "wars of the carrion and the spiders" which were being waged outside him. It is not easy to say why he never continued to write poetry. He said himself that scholarship claimed him too ardently, and there was no time for poetry, that it was impossible to concentrate on the problems before him at a time when the whole country was in upheaval. He had always written with difficulty, stripping himself for the combat like an athlete, and when the time came to put a seal on his poetic works, it was done gracefully, without ambiguity and with the studied temper of a man relinquishing poetry for ever:

> He, who night and morning, asks God for grace and not for gifts, who fills his day with the study of a good book or conversation with a thoughtful friend: such a man is freed from the slavery of hope and fear—the hope of rising, the fear of falling—lord not of lands, but of himself; and though without wealth or possessions, yet having all that the heart of man need desire.

The original lines are in verse, but it has seemed better to translate them into prose, for fear that anything might be added, when so much has already been taken away. There is a gravity in his writing, a deep and abiding sympathy for the people, which gives him an importance which none of the early renaissance poets possessed. His poem *The Heart Beats* might have been written by Tu Fu. *The Deserted Village* is only one of a long line of poems written to celebrate a perpetually barren countryside. His scenes are of rocks and gorges, of slow tempests and long wars, of an incessant search after a faith which had been denied to him. In one of the later poems he renounced even the effort of faith in a passionate renunciation which gains strength from its very weakness. It is the cry of a child at night who is not afraid of the dark but knows that it will last for ever:

You swear by the sun, and you call on the swans to witness
Your proclamation of faith. Well, I believe you entirely,
Even if your love blossoms into tears, I shall not be surprised,
But to say it will survive the sea and the land—
That makes me laugh to death! Surely I should be satisfied
With this breathing-spell of love's drunkenness?
What need is there to say "forever" and "eternity"?
Love, you know, I have only the ambition of the moment.
Come, embrace my heart quickly, but go if you want to go! . . .

Against the dark, against those who refuse (in the phrase of Kierkegaard) to exist in "the instant of delight", Wen Yi-tuo had neither pity nor scorn nor indifference, but only a childlike faith and a savage hope in the future. The savagery is there—it can be seen in a poem like *Early Summer Night* and in the essay which is included at the end of this book where he insists on the values of emotions undiluted by civilisation—but it is restrained by a natural sympathy for people, whose despairs are not unlike his own. The peasants die. The soldiers go down between the lanes of poplars to the wars, and in his imagination they are continually dying, though he sees them living before his eyes. China, a country where catastrophes happen with the same orderly progress as the seasons, can no longer be cured by the ancient virtues of the Confucian scholars, or even by exile in taoist nonconformity. He seems to see no hope for the future except in a race which is born again, fresh and untrammelled by the age-old legacy of the past, clean, vigorous and strong. By leading the great march of the Chinese Universities from Peking to the south-west, he had done more than most to bring that race into being.

The titles of those early collections of poetry are sometimes as revealing as the poems themselves. Hsu Chih-mo's *Small Letters to Loving Eyebrows, Looking Northwards, The Tiger, Wanderings in the Clouds* express an essential discontent and a wandering glance towards the past. Wen Yi-tuo's *Red Candles* and *Dead Water* even more obviously express the change in mood from romantic acceptance to a defiant renunciation. Pin Hsing's volume of verses could only have been called *Spring Water*. There was an elegance in those early poems which is lacking in the poems written in the full tide of war, but it was a necessary elegance. Pien Chih-lin, using forms founded on French models, was to give it depth and sonority. Feng Chih was to carve out with it a kingdom of his own, and Ho Chih-fang was to discover with it dark landscapes which had never been seen before. Even Ai Ching seems at times to have been influenced by the graces of these poets who seem to inhabit a world so utterly different from his own. The mood passed with the war, but with its passing there went the last vestige of the old splendours. Henceforward, poetry was to become the rugged thing the experimenters feared above all things: a thing of sticks and stones, broken hopes, the murderous hatred against the Japanese.

II

Since the day when Yen Fu first translated into *wen-li* the works of Montesquieu and Adam Smith, thus opening up the West to the Chinese, the Chinese scholars have thrown themselves into the task of understanding the West. They have usually failed, for the spirit of the West is not something that can be understood through translations alone, nor were the translations adequate to the needs of their readers, nor were they carefully chosen. The stream of translations which issued from the presses between 1887 and 1927 included many of the most important books of the West, but it included a larger majority of books whose importance was questionable. Karl Marx appeared, to be followed a little later by Rider Haggard. Homer made his appearance at the same time as Byron, and there was a period when Dumas' novels were held to be more revealing than Plutarch's *Lives*. Ibsen and Shaw followed, and their challenging calls to independence began to be heard in remote Chinese villages, where pale youths with pigtails studied them at night by the light of rapeseed oil-lamps. With the introduction of western literature, China changed beyond recognition, and the death-blow to the Manchu Empire was given, not by Sun Yat-sen, but by the obscure scholar who translated into impeccable literary Chinese *The Wealth of Nations* and *The Essay on the Laws*.

The revolution which Yen Fu brought about might have been more successful if the books had been chosen with a greater understanding of the spirit of the West. There was no universal arbiter to tell the Chinese who was worth reading, and who had contributed largely to the ethics of the West. For years the great story-writer Lu Hsun was under the impression that Maurus Jokai was the greatest novelist produced in the West, and even to-day Washington Irving is considered by many scholars who should know better as the prototype of all that is best in American literature. Because so many books had been translated in so short a time, there grew up among young scholars a confused picture of a West riddled with heroes and made black with poverty, a country where Achilles still rode out to make war on Hector and Karl Marx still inveighed against the evils of the capitalist state. The thirty centuries of western literature were compressed into a single moment of vision, and the height of scholarship was to be able to understand the complex forces which had brought this moment about.

Among those who attempted within the limits of a single lifetime to exhaust all the treasures of the West was a young scholar educated in Japan called Kuo Mo-jo. He possessed the quick wits of the Szechuanese, a fierce pride and an unruly temper. More important perhaps than any of these, he possessed a determination to reveal the West to the Chinese with a completeness which had never been attempted before. He translated *War and Peace*, several of Upton Sinclair's novels, the *Rubáiyát* of Omar Khayyàm, great quantities of Shelley's poetry, the whole of *Faust* and *The Sorrows of Werther*, and so many minor works that he has himself lost count of the number of books he has translated. There is only one objection to these translations: nearly all of them are made from the Japanese. Kuo Mo-jo was not alone in this curious experiment. Lu Hsun's translations of Gogol, Chao Ching-shen's translations of Chekhov and a thousand others were all made from the Japanese, and suffered inevitably from the refraction which occurs when an intense beam of light passes through two layers of coloured water. Against this background of unassimilated knowledge, Kuo Mo-jo advanced theories about the West, which seemed strange to the members of the Crescent Society, who had seen the West in all its misery and glory. He became a socialist, and later a communist. He wrote voluminously in a short jagged prose which reflects perfectly many of the spiritual indecisions of the time. "When I am carried away by my emotions," he wrote, "I am like a galloping horse, but when my emotions die down, I am like a burst porpoise." He wrote poetry, founded the Creation Society in opposition to the Crescent Society and made plans for a complete translation of Goethe. Forced to flee to Japan, he developed an interest in classical Chinese literature and like Wen Yi-tuo, but with far less skill, developed theories on the books contained in the Confucian canon. He wrote a play on the tragic death of Chu Yuan, and when the Nanking Government was transferred to Chungking he assumed the post of Director-General of Propaganda among the Forces.

As a poet he was a portent of the times. His strident, emotional versification makes demands on the reader which are often greater than the reader is able to bear. He writes because writing is in his blood, but also because he suffers from an intense desire for self-dramatisation: the members of the

Crescent Society outlawed "self-expression" and lifted art on the throne of pure worship. Kuo Mo-jo placed self-expression on the throne, worshipped it and cared less than nothing for the purity of the language. His importance lies in what he attempted to do rather than in anything he has performed. Yet he possesses considerable power, and though none of his poems have been included here, because it is almost impossible and hardly worth while to translate them into English, it would be a mistake to omit his name altogether. He represents in embryo much that was later to grow to fruition in Ai Ching and Tien Chien, the two poets who are most representative of the war.

With the advent of Ai Ching, we come at last to the parting of the ways. Once again, as in Confucius' time, poetry becomes in his hands a revelation of the country's rude health. Belonging to no school, subscribing to no poetic laws, a southerner who has made his home in the north, he was the first to perform the essential poetical and surgical operation of completely separating Chinese poetry from its roots in the past and transplanting them in the soil. It is a poetry of earth, of the things that happen on the earth, sketched out against the immense northern skies. He is almost independent of all influences. In him you hear the earth singing, the desolate cries of the birds as they wing their way across the plains. He can describe all the sorrow and sadness of China in a single line. "Verhaeren is my favourite poet," he once wrote, "as Van Gogh is my favourite painter. Verhaeren's poems are full of a deep knowledge of human society: he knows the hearts of modern men and the more passionate and complicated emotions which are arising now for the first time. I have no love for the romantic poets. I have no affection for Goethe's self-conceit, nor for his preaching, though it is clear to me that he is great. I love Shakespeare's *Hamlet*, which I have read several times. Of Mayakovsky I like only the early poem *The Cloud in Trousers*—his other poems seem to me vapid from too much exaggeration." But what is surprising in this statement is that he seems to have been influenced by none of the poets he mentions, and least of all by Verhaeren. Only Van Gogh seems to have influenced him, for the same sun which flamed over the wheatfields of Arles shines in his poetry over the plains of north China. There is something in him of Antonio Machado, whose bleak categories of the Spanish deserts are perfectly represented in Ai Ching's shorter poems, and perhaps it is inevitable that Spain and China, the two angels standing at the gates of the vast continent of Eden, should produce the same kind of barren, hard-bitten and superbly desolate poetry.

Like Po Chu-I, the famous old poet of the T'ang Dynasty, Ai Ching is fond of reading his poems aloud to old servants and workmen. The weakness of his poetry lies in its repetition and in the fact that the emotion is often deliberately limited to the least common multiple of his audience. He is always the propagandist, even when he praises the sun. "I sing because I am alive," he once wrote. "The rhythms of poetry are the rhythms of life, and the syllables of poetry are the beat of life." Life flows urgently through his poetry, and he is apt to find poetry where no one has noticed it before. "Once I came upon a notice in a printing shop. It was a notice written by one workman to warn another, and said: 'Ai Ming, remember that car.' That was all, but it seemed to me that the notice was deeply beautiful and the man who wrote it was a great genius of poetry." But neither Ai Ming nor the car, though they rhyme in Chinese, possess universal significance, and there are moments when Ai Ching verges dangerously on the ridiculous, especially when he addresses the sun in the same tones of earnest exhortation. What remains is his perfect ear, his deep sympathy for the people and for the deserts of north China, and like a god he peoples its emptiness with his dreams.

Perhaps it is no accident that two of the greatest poets of modern China were first painters, and that both were attracted to the Impressionists, for China in a very particular sense is a country which can only be understood through *impressions*. No dialectic is possible, and no severe metaphysics are endurable in a country so changeful. It is a country where the apothegm and the annotation take the place of philosophical symbols, where all that can be remembered of so long a past is a series of anecdotes, nearly all of them probably untrue. The man who would attempt to describe China must deal in violently contrasting brush-strokes, setting up his canvas in such a way that nothing is harmonised on a close view, but everything is harmonised at a distance of three paces or so. The impressionist painter is the key to modern Chinese painting, which oddly copies the excesses of Matisse, but he is also the key to modern Chinese poetry, which descends from T'ang and Chou in much the same way as Cezanne descends from Leonardo da Vinci. Ai Ching describes the moment before the battle with something of the same pontifical grace which blossoms in the dynastic odes collected by Confucius:

> Listen, the deafening sound
> Thunders on the edge of Heaven.
> We breathe the mingled savours of earth and grass,
> And from a distance comes the odour of smoke.
> In trenches we spend our winters.
> Silently waiting for the command,
> Like a woman in labour
> Waiting patiently for the birth of her child,
> Our hearts, our breasts
> Flow with new abundant love:
> Now in these days approaching the end of life
> Which time has ordered for us,
> We prepare ourselves,
> Each one of us possessing a pure holy will,
> That we may deserve death in the glory of the battlefield
> —Ai Ching, *The Trumpeter*.

Here, as we might expect, nothing has changed: we are living in the same battle which obscured the kingdoms of Duke Wen more than twenty-five centuries ago. It is only later in the poem, when the young trumpeter is killed and his face is seen to be reflected on the silver metal of the trumpet that we realise that we have entered a more modern, a more disparate world. The old elegists would have been able to describe a whole battlefield in terms of a blood-stained flower or of a plume of smoke rising from the marsh-grass. Yet they would have found themselves incapable of the impressionist vision which sees all tragedy in the glint of a blood-smeared face on the reflecting surface of the trumpet, as the trumpeter lies dead. Impressionism had come to stay. It was the only way out, and it had the advantage of frail roots in the past—the poetry of Wang Wei, the sudden illuminations of Li Shang-yin, odd phrases here and there of Tu Fu and Li Po. The trumpeter dies—

> Silently he falls
> (No one has seen him fall)
> To the earth he adored above all things,
> His hand
> Still clasping the trumpet,
> And on the smooth metal of the trumpet
> Lies the reflection of his blood, his wan face,
> And there also are the advancing warriors,
> Their continual struggle,
> Horses neighing,
> Thundering war-chariots.
>
> And the sun, O the sun
> Glitters on the smooth metal. . . .

There is nothing else, but for the first time a symbol has been found which describes minutely and in the fewest possible strokes a whole battlefield. In a poem written about the mountain highways of the north, Ai Ching describes the winding roads as "strings tying up the whole earth". He has Tseng K'o-chia's peasant simplicity, but a finer artistry and a greater command of his material. *The Man Who Died a Second Time* is formless and hardly deserves the acclaim it received when it was first published, but how admirably he selects his material and how inevitably the soldier goes to his death! What is strange, and delightful, in Ai Ching is his power of giving universal significance to the things he describes, his sustained eloquence, his suggestions of the untamed wildernesses of the north. It has often been said that poetry springs on the verge between the desert and the sown; and this inhabitant of deserts who was born in the great sown lands of the south has more than any Chinese poet writing now the power to describe the abundant efflorescence of a new age. In *The Winter Forest, The Land Revived* and *The Words of the Sun* the earth itself seems to speak, quietly, in a mood of restrained eloquence and grace. We have to go back to *The Book of Songs* to find the simplicity which Ai Ching has brought to modern Chinese poetry.

III

In one of Tsao Yu's plays Peking Man, naked and beardless, the youth of the new age, bursts through the window and begins to hurl abuse at the family of an old Mandarin in Peking. Something similar to this happened when the longer pieces of Tien Chien were first published. The simplicity of Tien Chien goes beyond the simplicity of Ai Ching. In the words of an essay by Wen Yi-tuo which has already become famous: "Here there is not only the music of the drum but also the emotion of the drum, the same sound which is heard . . . in Eugene O'Neill's 'Emperor Jones', the mad African drum crackling with heat and the energy of life." With Tien

Chien we enter a world which passes almost beyond poetry altogether, a world of simple hammer-beats, of emotion untrammelled by complexity, a world where there are no lute players, no deceits, no diplomatic manœuvres, where there is nothing but clear honesty and purpose, vigorous life and the unending pursuit of good, and all this expressed in the simplest possible and the most resounding terms.

The phenomenon of Ai Ching owes everything to the war: Tien Chien seems to belong to no time or place. There is a directness of rhythmical effect in his poetry which can only be compared with the third part of T. S. Eliot's *The Waste Land* or the old latin hymn of the *Aval Brotherhood* sung by the priests of Mars:

> Enos Lares iuuate
> Neue lue rue Marmar sins incurrere in pleores
> Satur fu fere Mars limen sali sta berber
> Semunis alternei aduocapit conctos
> Enos Marmor iuuate
> Triumpe triumpe triumpe triumpe triumpe,[1]

where the heavy double beat of the first line thrice repeated followed by the quickening rhythm of the second and the running triplets of the third give the words an immediacy of effect which seems to spring from some equation between the rhythm of the song and the rhythm of our pulse-beats. There are ultimate rhythms, so simple that we have almost forgotten them, and it is with these ultimate rhythms that Tien Chien acquires his prodigious and untranslatable effects.

[1] Help us, O lares,
Let not plague or ruin, O Mars, fall upon the multitude!
Be content, fierce Mars, leap the threshold, halt, strike.
Summon in turn all the gods of sowing.
Help us, O Mars.
Leap! Leap! Leap! Leap! Leap!

The significance of Tien Chien is that he has opened up an entirely new field of poetry, where the drum, the heart-beat and the pulse acquire an importance which they never acquired before. The monosyllabic, or disyllabic Chinese tongue offers extraordinary possibilities to a poet determined to sing *without breath*, with the whole body rather than with the voice alone, with the effortless spontaneity of the whole physical complex rather than with some small part of it. The style he has hammered out of the Chinese language is unlike anything that has been seen before. Reading Tien Chien, there are moments when even Ai Ching appears to be following the traditional stream of Chinese poetry, when Pien Chih-lin might almost appear to be a survival from the T'ang Dynasty. With Tien Chien we are on completely new ground—the world of the immediate present, steel-like, rigorous, fresh like the dawn.

The quality chiefly noticeable in Tien Chien's poetry, apart from its extremely complex simplicity, is a sense of purely physical exaltation. He delights in life. He delights in the dance, and most of all (since he is a poet) in the almost animal-like cries which the dancers give off in their happiness. The world he lives in may be compared with the barbaric dances of *Prince Igor* or with the world of Emperor Jones where, according to the statement of the author, the beat of the tom-tom starts "at a rate exactly corresponding to the normal pulse-beat—72 to the minute—and continues at a gradually accelerating rate from this point uninterruptedly to the end of the play". But what is strange in the world of Tien Chien is that in spite of the barbaric rhythms of his longer pieces, everything takes place in an atmosphere of pure lucidity and bright sunlight. In the shorter pieces, where he seems to be most at his ease, there is no obstruction between emotion and the pure expression of emotion: the words flow from him as they flow from a child. He likes to use onomatopoetic words, and in this he is following the most ancient Chinese usage, for

The Book of Songs is filled with the reduplicative characters which imitate the sounds of birds or the tinkle of jade girdle-pendants; but he uses them with tremendous force. It is quite impossible to render his poems into English with success, but something of the crystalline light which flows through him and of his use of a rhythmless hammer-beat style can be seen in the following poem from his earliest collection:

THE SONG OF DAWN

I hear
The eastern wood
Is awake.

The dead sun creeps
Along
The length of the unflowing
Abyss,
Where the Siberian
Prisoners
Open their eyes,
Washing
Their lousy hair.
Nature sings sweetly,
Farmers sow
Golden seeds
On the desolate earth.
A definite beauty
Is born.
The people cry:
To-day
Everything is extraordinary!

The "definite beauty" which arises from so simple a poem is not achieved without great difficulty. These poems owe little enough to Mayakovsky, and more than Tien Chien sometimes seems to suspect from the genius of the Chinese language, with its high-pitched single tones and curious overtones of sound; for a Chinese scholar reading a Chinese poem aloud soon finds himself singing falsetto, and the waves of sound from a single word will pursue all the succeeding waves to the end. So it is with Tien Chien, who employs every conceivable trick of suspense and hesitation by shortening his lines while yet lengthening to an almost inconceivable degree the underlying flow of the paragraph. "Lines should stop according to men's breaths," he wrote, "or according to the content of ideas, but rhythms belong to the written word." For him the written word is the enemy: it must leap and dance on the page, it must be made to glow, it must be hammered into physical shape until you can take it up in your hands, drop it on the page and hear it ringing. There are times, however, when his simplicity defeats itself, and there exists a curious poem which he wrote one morning in Shansi when his commander rode away to a neighbouring villa in search of news:

> He rode away on his horse,
> He rode away. . .
>
> Smiling face
> Against the strong wind and sand.
>
> At evening
> He will return,
>
> Bringing news,
> Bringing food.

It is clear that Tien Chien's method suffers from serious limitations, and can only be used when the poetic theme possesses significance. Reading him in English, the reader should imagine that in place of each word there is a Chinese character, and in place of each sound there is heard the plucking of a violin-string, and he should remember too the accumulative effect of these sudden sounds swiftly following upon one another, racing towards a known conclusion, continually moving and yet continually still. Something of the same effect can be heard when you listen to a Chinese violin imitating the sounds of warriors fighting. The music of the violin is at first so delicate that it seems impossible to believe that it can convey the noises of the battlefield, but as the tempo increases in violence these faint dissonances take on the character of the heaviest sounds, they have weight and power, and you have only to close your eyes and you are in the midst of the battle. Tien Chien achieves the same effect by the overwhelming accumulation of short lines, each followed by a short pause; and though the English version of the long fragment included here fails precisely because the English language lacks so many qualities of the Chinese, something of the poet's achievements should at least be visible between the lines.

Tien Chien is the last of the revolutionaries, for it seems impossible to believe that the revolution can go farther. Throughout the long history of Chinese poetry evocation and suggestion have been the means towards an end of pure beauty. "Poetry is teaching," wrote Confucius, but few paid attention to him. With Tien Chien poetry is reduced to the starkest possible rhythmical statement, and in its bleak merciless outlines we see the figure of the young China, untrammelled by the past, forging into a new future. We may regret his existence, and there are not many who will entirely agree with Wen Yi-tuo's essay, but in this age and at this time it would be dangerous to regret his power. If poetry is teaching, he has found an instrument through which his teaching may be heard, and he has done one thing which no one else has done before him—he has released the energy concealed in the formal pattern of the Chinese character until, like an explosion, it bursts from the page.

IV

The main lines of modern Chinese poetry run through Wen Yi-tuo, Ai Ching and Tien Chien, but there were others whose importance in developing the traditional themes, Pien Chih-lin, Feng Chih and Ho Chih-fang particularly, should not be under-estimated. Pien Chih-lin has the slow unhurried explorative gaze of the old scholars, and a kind of delicacy so superbly controlled that it is difficult to realise that he holds himself on a knife-edge balance between East and West. He has read everything and forgotten nothing. He has translated at least forty books, and he has always translated the books he likes best. Saturated in the French symbolists, in the novels of Henry James, in Spender and Auden (whom he worships with an almost childlike glee), he speaks with an individual voice which owes very little to the foreigners he has read and nearly everything to the Chinese tradition. Even when he is half-quoting Eliot:

> The road stretching to the evening resembles a stretch of desperation,

he is still wholly himself, and the road he describes is not the road which passes through Jerusalem, but that far longer and more difficult road which the Chinese call *Tao*. He is superb in his short pieces, for he has a fragmentary vision of life—refusing to believe that we can see more than the fragments—and perhaps it is as a result of this that he so often gives the impression of vast spaces and deserts:

> Like a man in middle-age
> I look back on the traces of the past,
> Every step a desert.
> Waking out of a strange dream,
> I hear the crows of evening over half the sky.

In Pien Chih-lin the broken edges never meet to form a perfect circle, and it is only rarely, as in *Peking City*, that he can launch himself into a world where the fragments have less importance than the whole. In the coldly calculated hysteria of this poem the whole of Peking comes before our eyes. Written in the enervating Spring of 1934, when the Japanese were at the gates, the mood of subtle acquiescence and horror are caught perfectly in the images of the glazed tiles and flying kites, and the swelling irony against the city which refused to defend itself mounts with the deliberately slangy rhythms. I do not know any poem by a modern Chinese poet which is quite so successful as this one.

Perhaps the modern poet to whom Pien Chih-lin bears the most resemblance is Boris Pasternak, who also fell under the influence of Rainer Maria Rilke. Sometimes he gives the impression of a diver leaping from an immense height into the depths of an immensely deep sea, which he explores more thoroughly than any other poet before him. The sea, the air, the mountains and the rivers of China are seen through his eyes, and possess the clarity and depth and continual movement of a T'ang Dynasty painting. His images are concrete and his people are living in exactly the same way that the images and people of a Chinese painting are living, caught in a casual mood of sustained eloquence and gravity, when they are least conscious of being seen. The girl in *The Broken Ship* belongs to heraldry:

> The tide is flowing in. The wave offers her
> A piece of broken ship. Without saying a word,
> She resumes her place on the rock.
> Let the setting sun paint the shadow of her hair
> On the piece of a broken ship. Long, and long after
> She will look again to the edge of a vast sea:
> She will not find the white sail she has seen before.
> The tide ebbs, but she will not send
> The piece of the broken ship into the sea.

This is all, but a whole world has been brought to life, a whole race is suggested by the figure of the solitary girl, and perhaps a whole civilisation is accused. One may compare this poem with one of the last sonnets of Feng Chih:

> From the uncertain streams
> One carries back a bottle full of water,
> And thereby the water acquires a definite form.
> See, the flag floating in the autumn wind
>
> Attempts to hold something which cannot be held:
> Distant dark nights, glimmering sparks,
> The growth and decay of unseen herbs,
> Hearts and minds racing forever into the distance...

where the vase and the flag are in the same way symbols of reality, the vase almost identical with the girl and the flag almost identical with the piece of a broken ship. Comparing them, we notice how the ancient symbols are replaced by symbols with a more exacting meaning, and how there will always be a place, in spite of the irruptions of Tien Chien, for the poetry of delicate sustained feeling. The mood and the manner will change, but the main current of the ancient poetry will remain, and perhaps inevitably there will be two poetries, the one bright with the glory of the future and the other still brighter with the unfading honour of the past.

There is one poet, not included here, who might have been able to rival Tien Chien if he had lived long enough. He died in 1935 after swallowing a fish-bone, an end which would have amused his bright ironic mind. Only two collections of his work have appeared, the first published in 1936 called *Our Castle*, and the second called *Roaring*, published some years later. In the wilderness of his wild poetry there is much tenderness, and a great deal of unnecessary violence, but there is one poem which seems to suggest, as no other poem included here does, the particular feeling of the Chinese for the new age which has descended upon them. It is here translated directly into prose:

> "The blood becomes wine, becomes cigarettes, changes into motor-cars, changes into chains round our necks. Our bones are material for joining flower-cars, for building up skyscrapers, for making golden palaces. The flesh feeds the peony, and little dogs feed on flesh as on rice. There are the happy and the poor, only these. Laughter buries thousands. Happiness causes the misfortunes of millions. A group of people dying is due to many living. Sweet songs establish the mourning and crying of the poor." (Wang Den, *The Roaring*.)

Even though it is in prose, I think it is possible to see the passion behind it, the controlled fury of the mind which wrote so steadily and so worthily, and which discovered in the vision of Shanghai a sense of desolate brotherhood with the poor. In the past too few Chinese poets concerned themselves with the poor, and Tu Fu alone of the great poets has uttered his condemnation of all governments which allow the poor to remain. What is essential is that Chinese poetry should not altogether surrender to politics, nor should it be wholly immersed in a contemplation of beauty, and in Ai Ching, Tien Chien and Wen Yi-tuo, and in many other of the poets collected here, there is a balance which defies analysis, but which suggests that there is the same spiritual health among the younger Chinese poets as there is among the professors, who first taught that Chinese poetry need not follow along the paths laid down in the Han Dynasty. The explosive violence of Tien Chien is here to stay, but along with it there remains, perpetuated through the centuries and always changing, the still more explosive quietness of the poets who are determined to retain whatever is good of the ancient Chinese traditions.

ROBERT PAYNE.

HSU CHIH-MO

HSU CHIH-MO *was not perhaps the greatest of modern poets, but long after his death in an airplane accident at Tsinanfu in 1931, he remains the most beloved. He was tall and handsome, slightly notorious for his love affairs, the son of a rich merchant whose greatest desire was that his son should follow in his footsteps. Hsu Chih-mo refused, entered Peking University and became the first serious exponent of modern Chinese poetry, giving it grace and imaginative power, and continually experimenting in the use of unfamiliar forms. His debt to Shelley and Whitman was great, but still greater was the debt he owed to the small circle of poetic investigators who called themselves the* Crescent Society. *It was a society which Hsu Chih-mo held together by his charm and wit, and by the enduring qualities of his own understanding of poetry. In a verse written shortly before his death, he said: "I shall die against the Great Mountain." His death when hurrying to meet his mistress in Peking assumed a symbolic character in the eyes of the young, and in those who believe in the curious fatality of dates; for in 1931 Japan invaded Manchuria and the young Chinese could no longer write about love affairs and in the beauty of maidens' eyes. He who loved birds and airplanes fell from the clouds when his airplane crashed into a foggy mountainside on an otherwise bright summer day.*

He was born in 1895 in Chia-shih district, in Chekiang. After leaving Peking University he went to Columbia University and later to King's College, Cambridge, where he failed to take a degree, but met Katharine Mansfield and Middleton Murray, both of whom formed a lasting impression on him. For a while he worshipped before the throne of E. M. Foster, who has since described his meeting with the young poet as one of the most exciting things that happened to him. Returning to China and teaching at Tsinan University in Chekiang, and later at the Central University in Nanking, he continued to contribute to the Crescent Monthly, *but seems to have been homesick for Peking and for Cambridge. He returned at last to Peking to accept a professorship at Peking University; wrote feverishly and lived violently, at the mercy of his own presentiment of his death; and was probably on the verge of great poetic discoveries at the moment when he died. He left at least eight collections of poetry and a vast collection of unedited essays. His collections include:* Poems of Chih-mo, *1925*, A Night in Florence, *1926*, The Tiger, *1930*, Wanderings in the Clouds, *1931*.

FAREWELL TO CAMBRIDGE

Silently I go,
As silently I came.
Silently I wave my hand
And bid farewell to the western clouds.

The golden willows on the river bank
Are brides beneath the setting sun:
Their flaming shadows in the wave's light
Move softly on my heart.

Green weed in soft clay,
Greenly tossing beneath the water:
In the soft waves of Cam
I am content to be a weed.

The pool under the elms' shadow
Is not a clear spring, but a rainbow
Shattered among pondweeds,
Falling at last into rainbow dreams.

Who seeks dreams? Poling a long pole,
Roving through places greener than green grass,
A boat fully loaded with starlight
Sings beneath splendid stars.

Now I cannot sing aloud,
And silent are the farewell flutes:
Even the insects are silent for me
On this silent Cambridge night.

Silently I go,
As silently I came.
I wave my sleeves,
Carrying away no silk of clouds.

A SONG OF THE SEA

I

"Girl, girl alone,
Why do you wander
The twilight shore?—
Girl, go home, girl!"

"No, I won't go!
Let the evening wind blow
On the sands, in the glow.
My hair is combed by the winds,
As I wander to and fro."

II

"Girl with the hair uncombed,
Why do you stay
By the cold silent sea?
Girl, go home, girl!"

"No, let me sing,
Let me sing, wild sea who sings to me.
Under the starlight, in the cool winds
A girl's voice singing free."

III

"Girl, daring girl,
Dark clouds are coming over the sea's edge.
Soon there will be fierce clouds.
Girl, go home, go!"

"Look, I am dancing in the air,
I am a seagull dancing among waves,
In the evening tide, in the sands,
Swiftly hovering, gracefully,
Back and forth, back and forth."

IV

"Hark, the wild rages of the wild sea!
Girl, go home, go!
Look, the waves are fierce beasts.
Girl, go home, girl!"

"The waves will not eat me,
I am like the tossing of the wild sea!
In the tide's song, in the wave's light
I hurry amidst the sea-foam,
Tumbling, tumbling!"

V

"Girl, where are you, girl?
Where is your song?
Where is your graceful body?
Where are you, daring one?"

The dark night eats up all the stars.
There is no more light on the sea,
No more girl on the beach,
No more girl—no—

FOLLOW ME

THE world is afraid,
Intolerant of love, intolerant of love!
Loosen your hair,
Bare your feet,
Follow me, my love!
Abandon this world,
Let us die for our love.
Let me hold your hand,
Follow me!

Let thorns pierce through our feet,
Let hailstorms break open our heads,
Follow me!
Let me hold your hand!
Come, let us escape into freedom!

Follow me, my love:
The world has dropped behind,
Look, the white sea,
The boundless wild sea
Leading into freedom.
Let us make love in this freedom!

Look where my hand is pointing!
There is a blue sky, a blue star,
There is an island with green grasses,
There are flowers, beasts, beautiful birds:
Come, take the small ship,
Sail to Eden,
Love, happiness and freedom.
Come, let us leave the world behind!

THE SNOW

If I were the snow
Fluttering to and fro,
I must know where to go.
Flying, flying, flying—
Where shall I go?

Not in some hidden vale,
Not in a lonely dale,
Nor alone in an unknown road—

Flying, flying, flying—
This is how I shall go!

I shall dance gracefully in the air,
I shall know perfectly the air's tranquil dwelling-place,
I shall look down upon gardens—
Flying, flying, flying—
Breathing the crystal perfume of the plum-tree!
So light in the air
That I can fall against her dress,
Creeping close to her heart,
Melting, melting, melting—
Melting into her soft breast!

LOVE

Love, who is he?
I was not born when he came.
For twenty years the sun shone over me.
I was a child, knew nothing of pain,
Until on that day, so beloved and hated,
My heart was in sad toils. I knew something was wrong.
For the first time in my life I was imprisoned.
They said I was wounded—please, feel my heart-strings.
I was not born when he came.
Love, who is he?

I became an untamed horse,
Galloping the vast wilderness of life.
I was the old man of Ch'u who held the imprisoned jewel,[1]

[1] Refers to the ancient legend of a man from Ch'u in modern Hunan who discovered a jewel hidden in a stone and offered it to the Emperor. The Emperor refused the gift, saying no jewel was hidden in it, till the man hurled the stone on the ground and the jewel was revealed.

Pointing to his heart, saying: "Here is the best jewel of all."
If you don't believe me, plunge a knife in my breast
And see whether a handful of bleeding flesh is a jewel or not.
Blood, the merciless knife-thrust, O my soul!
Who compelled me to ask this question of life?

Ah, but now I am awake and happy in my wakefulness.
God, I am no longer sick, I won't groan any more.
I no longer desire to live in cloudland,
I only want the earth, content to be a common man,
No longer asking who love is.
I was not born when he came.

THE BEGGAR

"Kind lady, kind gentleman, give me a dime."
   The north-west wind cut his face like a knife.
"Give me a scrap of food for my dinner."
   The dark shadow leaned close to the great door.

"Kind gentleman, you who are rich, I am starving."
   From within came laughter: red stoves, decorated cups.
"Kind gentleman, listen, I am frozen and starving to death."
   The north-west wind laughed: "To hell with you, beggar!"

What am I? I am a bundle of cowering shadow
   Shuddering in the cold of a long street.
I desire only such warmth and sympathy
   As will shelter my bruised bones and crushed flesh.

A voice from the closed door says: "How dare you?"
The north-west wind screams: "To hell with you, beggar!"

ON LISTENING TO THE BELLS OF TIEN-NING TEMPLE, CHIEN CHOW

As though in the sunshine, lovely as fire, lying among the tangled grasses and listening to the first summer songs of the partridges as they ring from the zenith of the sky straight into the clouds and back from the clouds into the zenith of the sky;

As though in the moonlit desert, the soft fingers of the moon touching one by one the sun-stricken sands, in the tropic air soft and slippery as swansdown, gently, gently ringing from afar, drawing nearer, then drifting away again;

As though in a deserted valley, when the evening star shines lonely above the world with the light of a burnt-out sun, and the wild grasses and the wild trees pray in utter solitude, and then hearing a blind man sounding his fortune-teller's gong and holding a young boy by the hand, and the sound of the gong echoing and re-echoing through a darkened world;

As though on a rock by the sea, where the waves leap like tigers, and the sky bursts through the heavy curtain of dark clouds, and listening to the voice of the sea, the threatening and repenting storms, the soft voice of the sea speaking of her sins;

As though on the white summits of the Himalayas, listening to the footsteps of wind reverberating among innumerable snow-white precipices;

So I have heard the tolling bells of Tien-Ning Temple.

Whence comes this god? Is there such a thing on the earth?

Beating of bells, drums, wooden fishes, praying and psalms . . . A symphony reverberating in the great temple and through the universe, slowly and haltingly reverberating, so that innumerable conflicts are harmonised and innumerable opposing colours are purified and innumerable divergencies are extinguished;

Praying and psalms, the beating of bells, drums, wooden fishes, the harmony reverberating through the universe, unloosening a little dust of Time and enclosing the cause and effect of countless centuries;

Whence comes this great symphony. . . . Splendours of seas of stars, the music of the spheres, flooding tides of life, all movement ceasing, ceasing. . .

At the ends of the earth and the sky, among the gold-lit temples, in my ears, in my senses, in my heart, in my dreams. . .

In dreams, in the momentary revelations, in the blue sky, in the white waters, in the softness of green grass: in the homeland. . .

The wings of light flying in immensity!

Ecstasy flowing from the divine truth, and harmonised in the silence and boundlessness and solemnity of serenity. . .

Praise, O God, praise, praise, praise. . .

ONE NIGHT AT FLORENCE

So you are really leaving to-morrow? Well . . .
Don't worry at all, sooner or later there is always a day of departure.
If you want to remember me, well, remember me,
But if you don't—forget me, if it is not too late.
Don't worry your head over me . . .
Remember it was like a dream, something dream-like
Like the broken blossoms we saw on the road yesterday

Trembling in the wind . . .
Two blossoms trembling, fallen, trampled in the mud . . .
Trodden down . . . coated with mud . . . becoming mud . . .
This state of half-living, half-dying is truly intolerable,
This being miserable, this worrying, this courting the contempt
    of friends . . .
Heavens, why should you be so . . . why should you . . .
I cannot forget you. The day you came
Was like lightning shining on a dark future . . .
You are my teacher, my lover, my benefactor . . .
You taught me what life is, what love is,
You awakened me from my stupor, gave me my innocence back
    again.
Without you, how could I know the sky was so high or the
    grass so green?
Touch my heart: see how fast it is beating.
Touch my face: see how fearfully it is burning.
Unfortunately you cannot see in this darkness.
My love, I can scarcely endure these flames.
Don't kiss me. My soul is like iron in a furnace, being stricken
    under the hammer of love, stricken, stricken. . . .
Shedding of sparks. I faint. Hold me.
O love, let me in this quiet garden
Close my eyelids, die against your breast, O beautiful!

The winds sigh in the poplars.
This is my elegy, spoken on the silent wind,
Blown from the olives, scented with the fragrance of pome-
    granates,
Carrying my soul away. Here the glow-worm
Tenderly lights my way.
I'll stop at the camel bridge with the three archways,
Listening to you as you embrace my cold body,
Calling me sadly, kissing me, shaking me. . . .
I shall follow the wind to the end,

And whether it leads me to Heaven or Hell, I shall not care.
I have abandoned my life, I have come to "death in love",
And surely this "death in love" is five hundred times better
 than rebirth?
I know it is selfish, but what can I do?
Surely we should die together,
Flying together we should beat two pairs of wings:
Even in Heaven we shall have to care for each other.
I cannot be without you. Can you be without me? . . .
To live is hard: death cannot give me freedom,
And you should not sacrifice your freedom for me.
Alas! You tell me to wait, to wait for this day!
Is there such a day? My life lives in faith of you,
But you will leave when dawn breaks. How can you be so hard?

So you will really leave to-morrow? I cannot detain you,
But this flower without sunshine will never survive,
The petals will all wither away without your dew.
You cannot forget me, my love. I have no life except in you.
Yes, I will obey you, I will wait for the day,
When the iron-tree blossoms . . .
When I am dead, I shall become a glow-worm,
I shall lie in the garden, creeping among grass-roots, I shall fly
From evening to midnight, and from midnight to dawn,
Hoping there are no clouds that I may see the sky.
The great unchanging star in the sky will be you.
O, I beg you to shine and shower forth light through the night
So that you may touch always the secret heart of my love. . . .
Translated by Yuan K'o-chia.

WEN YI-TUO

UNTIL *recently, when he shaved off his brown and silver-streaked beard, he possessed all the benignity of the proverbial Chinese scholar; but with the end of the war against Japan, the promise made at the beginning of the war was redeemed, the beard came off, and the old scholar suddenly appeared to assume the guise of a young mechanic with a hard, clean face and a vigour which even typhus and continual poverty in an exiled Chinese University has done nothing to change. A giant among Chinese letters, he is famous as a seal-carver, as a paleographist, and for his revolutionary interpretations of the ancient Chinese classics, as well as for his poetry. He was the first to insist on an architectonic for modern Chinese poetry, the first to write modern Chinese poetry with grace and rigour. Though he is famous for his lectures on the* Book of Songs, *on Chuangtzu and the Confucian classics, he forms part of the advance guard which believes that China has everything to learn from the West and little enough from Confucius. Now Dean of the Department of Chinese letters at Tsinghua University, he is a fiery and dramatic speaker, worshipped by the students and justly hated by the reactionary elements in the country for his opposition to a Confucius-ridden system of graft and feudalism.*

He was born in 1898 in the province of Hupeh. Graduating in Tsinghua University, he studied painting at the Chicago Art Institute and the Art Students' League of New York. He confesses that he was not a good painter, but developed a love of colour which has remained throughout his life. His first volume of poems, Red Candles, *was published in 1922, to be followed six years later by the second and last volume,* The Dead Water. *He has since experimented in satiric poetry, but with the failure of the Great Revolution (1927-1929) and his self-imposed withdrawal from creative literature, it is unlikely that he will return to the field of his first love. He remains the scholar, perhaps the greatest and most representative, and certainly the most beloved in* modern China, with a scholar's ferocious desire for clarification. It is not for nothing that the greatest influences on his poetry have been French.

He has taught in nearly all the major Universities in China. For a period he was director of the National College of Fine Arts. Since then he has assumed the post of Dean of the Department of Foreign Languages at Central University, Nanking, and accepted chairs at Wuhan, Tsingtao, Tsinghua and Lienta.

This must be left as it stands, though Wen Yi-tuo was murdered by Kuomintang soldiers on July 15th, 1946 in Kunming, when he was about to return after an eight year exile to Peiping. He approved of the introduction six weeks before he died, smiling and a little dazed by the claims made for him, saying that he was the least of Chinese poets and if he wrote again he would write only with devastating satire. The murder of the students in December 1945 had made him sick at heart and more than ever determined to oppose the corruption of the government, conscious that in China this was the scholar's traditional task. Now, of all those who began the new movement in Chinese poetry, none survive.

A VASSAL

My Lord, I have come afar to pay you tribute,
Bringing you a shipload you have never seen,
And sure I am that you would love these gifts I send:
So I have journeyed with a joyful heart,
And scarcely do I know how you will take them.
They say there is no harbour now, all dried-up,
But I shall wait the swell of your tide of love
And float the full-bellied ship into your city,
Though the ratlines are dim, nothing carefully outlined,
And it was all shattered in a heedless moment.
I woke: I stood till moondown and till dawn,
But the new dream was unavailing,
And shattered was the old one.
So I failed to make good my dream.
Often the moon has waned, often flowers blossomed.
I have waited, waited in vain for the turn of the tide.
My lord, have we not heard the tide never fails?
Then how do I know when the ship comes home?

AUTUMN BEAUTY

The little stream is purple like grapes,
Scything up layers and layers of gold carp-scales.

A few maple-leaves shaped like scissors,
A few crimson swallows
Over the water
Hovering, soaring, diving, turning over and over . . .

The great maple leaves
Are fat, thick as bears' paws,
And they are scattered under the green window.
Nervous stealthy squirrels
Crawl in and out among the leaves,
Hunting for food against the coming cold.

The tall chestnut leaves
Complain the whole night against the cold east wind,
And have now at last found their freedom:
Their dry red faces
Smilingly bid farewell to ancient branches.

Piebald pigeons, white pigeons,
Silver-grey pigeons, pigeons with cornelian eyes,
Pigeons black as crows,
With purple-flushed feathers in a green-gold night—
All the pigeons tired of flying flock beneath the stairs,
Hiding beaks under wings,
Dozing peacefully.
A humid wind pervades the universe.
Three or four pert children
(Wearing orange, yellow and black velvet shirts)
Play in the hedges of cloves
Like goldfish playing among green reeds—
Surely they are sailing on the Huang-p'o river,
Those innumerable slender white poplars
Which stand out motionless against the night sky.

Enchanting green aspens: like young fops
Wrapped in gold-embroidered gowns.
One hand rests on their hips,
As they gaze down on the jade-green pond
Admiring their own reflections.

As they lean on crystal balustrades.
The smiling sun beams down on the world,
Smiling like gold—
Yellow gold smiling on fruit-trees,
Red gold smiling on oaks,
White gold smiling on the bark of pines.

These trees are no longer trees—
They are shining clouds
Of amber, of agate,
Clouds wafted by soft winds, shining in the morning sun!
These trees are no longer trees—
They are divine clouds!

These trees are no longer trees!
They are palaces in Peking
With green glass tiles,
With yellow glass tiles,
Pavilions built on pavilions,
Palaces built on Palaces . . .
Little birds singing with silvery voices,
But they are the tinkling of bells in the palaces.
These trees are no longer trees:
They are royal capitals glittering green and gold!

O, you multi-coloured Lord of Trees,
Neither the Lord of Ying Yang's embroideries,
Nor Turkish carpets,
Nor the Rose Window of Nôtre Dame,
Nor the frescoes of angels by Fra Angelico
Can compete with you in colours and freshness.
O, you multi-coloured autumn trees,
I envy your world of ease,
Your bohemian lives,
I envy your colours!

I desire the goddess to weave me an embroidered gown
So that I may adorn myself with your colours!
From grapes and oranges and stooks of yellow corn . . .
I desire to squeeze all colours, drink all colours!
With the poetry of Li Yi-shan and Keats[1]
I desire to sing your colours!
In Puccini's *La Boheme*,
In the paper-burning incense-pots made in Pao-san [2]
I even desire to listen to your colours,
Smell your colours!

I desire a life of colours
Like the multi-coloured autumn trees!

DEAD WATER

HERE is a ditch of dead and hopeless water:
No breeze can raise a ripple on it.
Best to throw in it scraps of rusty iron and copper,
And pour out in it the refuse of meat and soup.

Perhaps the copper will turn green as emeralds,
Perhaps the rusty iron will assume the shape of peach-blossoms.
Let grease weave a layer of silky gauze
And bacteria puff patches of cloud and haze.

So let the dead water ferment into green wine
Littered with floating pearls of white foam.
Small pearls cackle aloud and become big pearls,
Only to be burst like gnats to rob the vintage.

[1] Li Yi-shan, better known as Li Shang-yin, was a famous poet of the T'ang Dynasty.

[2] Pao-san in Shantung is well known for its pottery.

And so this ditch of dead and hopeless water
May boast a touch of brightness:
If the toads cannot endure the deadly silence,
The water may burst out singing.

Here is a ditch of dead and hopeless water,
A region where beauty can never stay.
Better abandon it to evil—
Then, perhaps, some beauty will come out of it.

PERHAPS

PERHAPS you are weary of weeping,
Perhaps you only want to sleep in peace:
Then bid the herons not cough,
The frogs not shout, and the bats stop wheeling.

Let the sunlight not pierce under eyelids,
Let the winds not stir your eyebrows,
For now no one may disturb you.
I bid the mountain god protect you.

Perhaps you can hear the earthworms toiling
And the frail roots of grass sucking water.
Perhaps you hear delicate music
More beautiful than earthly curses.

Therefore close tight your eyelids.
I'll let you sleep, I'll let you sleep.
I shall sprinkle yellow sand over you
And pray for paper money to float slowly over your grave.

CHESS-PLAYER

Beloved, you are the champion.
Come, let us play a game of chess.
To win you is not my aim.
My aim is to lose
My body and soul
Entirely within you.

THE CONFESSION

It's no joke at all, I'm not that sort of poet.
Though I adore the sheen of white quartz,
Though I love green pines, vast seas, the glimmer of sunset on
    a crow's back,
The dusky sky interwoven with the wings of bats,
Though I adore heroes and high mountains,
The flags of nations waving in the wind,
All colours from saffron to the heavy bronze of chrysanthemums,
Remember my food is a pot of old tea.

You should be afraid: there is another person in me:
His imagination is a gnat's and he crawls through muck.

THE LAST DAY

The dews were sobbing in the roof-gutters:
The white tongues of banana leaves lashed the glass pane.
Four white clay walls seem to be receding.
Alone I cannot fill the vast room.

A hearthful of flames is blazing in my heart,
While I await the call of a distant friend.
I add fuel to the flames—spiders' webs, rat dung,
The scales of snakes instead of chopped-up wood.

The cockcrow quickens the burning wood to ashes,
A gust of wind steals and gropes round my lips,
And then at last the stranger stands before me:
I close my eyes and follow him away.

I COME, I SHOUT . . .

I COME, I shout, I send you my tears and blood:
"This is not my country, this is not China—no!"
I have come because I heard your summons.
Running against the bitter wind, raising my torch high,
I come, now knowing that it is all in vain.
I have seen a nightmare, but you are not the nightmare.
This is horrible: a nightmare hanging over a cliff.
No, it is not you, my darling.
I ask from the heavens, and the wind blows from the four
    quarters.
I ask, and my fist drums the naked breast of the earth.
Still there is no news of you. I call you with my tears,
I pull out my heart and you are in my heart!

THE STREAM

THE leaden grey shadows of trees
Form a long volume of evil dreams,
Pressing heavily upon
The breast of the stream.
This wild stream struggles and struggles
And seems without influence . . .

THE HEART BEATS

The lamplight has whitened the walls,
The faithful tables and chairs are as intimate as friends,
There comes from the heaped books the smell of old paper,
My favourite cups look virtuous like virgins,
The baby presses his mouth against his mother's nipples,
From somewhere a snore proclaims the health of my eldest son.
O mysterious calm night, O perfect peace,
O voice of gratitude trembling in my throat!
And then once more the sweet damnable curse returns—
Calm night! No, I refuse to accept your bribes!
Who will fill the narrow space between these walls?
My world is larger and includes other worlds:
These walls cannot be separated from the agony of war.
How can you find a way to stop my heart beating?
Better to let my youth be filled with mud and sand
Than to praise one's own happiness and sufferings!
Better let rats dig deep holes in my skull,
Better let worms feed on the pulp of flesh and blood!
Once, did we live only for a cup of bread and for songs,
For the pleasant sound of the pendulum ticking in a calm night?
How did we hear the groans of our neighbours,
How could we see the shadows of the widows and orphans
    shivering against the wall,
Twitch of death in trenches, madmen biting their beds,
All these tragic scenes running under the mill of life.
Happiness! I shall not receive your bribes!
My world is not enclosed within these narrow walls.
Listen! The cannon-shot, the god of Death roaring!
O calm night, how can you stop my heart beating?

EARLY SUMMER NIGHT

The setting sun leaves the poet to the dreary night,
And he reminds her: "Reveal all your secret treasuries."
The violet sky spills broken pearls
And he believes they should be strung together
As adornments upon the breasts of death.

Claws of cold undertow comb the withered hair of starved willows,
Then wrings out their reflections from the pond in slivers of gold.
Half-way up the hill the falling cypress is hunchbacked:
Her dark, bony fists shake defiance at the sun.
The sleepless toads are overcome with their own weariness,
The village dogs bark in mournful, enquiring tones.
How can the nerves of thieves stand up to the strain?
A fire-swallowing, mist-spitting dragon climbs the iron stairway
With "War" engraved on the grey uniform, hoarsely shouting, sobbing.
The clapper of a great bell comforts the world,
Saying: "Sleep in peace," but who believes in the bell?
O God, knowing the pass the world has come to,
Are you not shuddering, O most benevolent God in the skies?

DEATH

O Death, soul of my soul,
Life of my life,
For my lifelong failures and lifelong debts:
For these only I seek satisfaction and retribution from thee!
(Since I have nothing else
To ask of thee.)

Let me be drowned in the brimming waves of thine eyes!
Let me be burned in the flaming fires of thy heart!
Let me be soaked in the sweet wine of thy voice!
Let me be suffocated in the scent of thy breath!

Else, let me be shamed to death by thy true dignity,
Let me be frozen to death in thy coldness.
Let me be bitten to death by the strength of thy fangs!
Let me be pierced to death by the steel-cold venomous sword!

If thou shalt favour me with happiness,
I shall die in happiness:
If thou shalt favour me with pain,
I shall die in pain.
Death is all that I beg of thee,
The supreme tribute I offer thee!

SPRING RAIN

THE cleansing rain is no more:
The thin mud everywhere bites into the soles of shoes.
Refreshing winds carry the smell of damp soil,
Probing our nostrils.

Certainly the goldfish do not fear the cold,
For all of them are floating on the surface.
The east wind patiently admonishes the cresses
To let the awakened shoots lift high their heads.

The spring rain is over. The shoots have risen an inch high,
Only to be swallowed up by the water in the pond.
Over the projecting roof-beams, over the projecting ledges
The elms are still lagging behind the spring,

Painted against the scales of a cloudy sky.
The sky is a sheet of paper, azure and white
On which the Monk Hwei Hsu in freehand
Once drew bold iron strokes, graceful hooks of silver.

The beanlike buds of the carnations
Are brimming with feverish life,
As they gaze on far horizons,
Reckoning on to-morrow's glories.
They are like poets pensively
Weaving their lines in clean air.
Spring, the open secret!
Divine magician—
I have lost myself in your mazes!
From now on I must exert all strength
That I may increase your amazing beauty
With my failing lines.

THE DESERTED VILLAGE

Where are they gone? What can the matter be
That toads squat on jars and lilies bloom on the ladles,
And tables and chairs and benches lie in the field furrows?
Rope-bridges of spiders-webs climb from east to west,
Coffins are stuck in the doorways, rocks block the windows—
How strange and how sad is the spectacle confronting me!
The scythes lie rusty in the soil,
The great fish-net lies decaying on the ash-pile.
Heavens, there is nothing to keep people in this fine village,
Where roses are forever blossoming, where water-lilies are like
    wide-open umbrellas,
Where the rice-shoots are slender and the lake is green,
And the sky is blue, and the birds sing like dew-pearls.

How did the rice-shoots get so green? Who asked the flowers
   to be so red?
With whose blood and whose sweat is the soil mingled?
Yet they went away resolutely, as though for good!
What griefs did they have? Why were they so determined?
Is there anything anyone could do? Tell them!
Hogs stray through the streets, ducks brush shoulders with pigs,
The peonies are trampled by cocks, the vegetables cropped by
   cows,
Tell them: At sunset the cattle have not come down from the
   hills.
There are only ghostly shadows, all of them waiting.
From all round the mountains reptiles and beasts are coming
   down,
If they knew this, surely a chill would travel up their spines,
They would droop their heads and never look up again.
Tell them this: The animals know
When night is coming down, when the aspens shake in the wind.
All they had to do was to bellow on the hill-top,
For though the passes were dangerous, their master would
   shepherd them home,
And the piping of flutes would lead them back to their sheds.
How sweet was the scent of hay, how warm the stable!
Thinking of this, how can they prevent their tears flowing
As they huddle together, jowl against jowl?
Go, tell your masters to return.
Tell them everything, do not hide anything.
Bid them return, bid them return immediately.
Ask them why they do not care for their cattle.
Don't they know that their cattle to them are as their children?
They are such poor creatures now, timid and shivering.
Tell me, where is the messenger who will go to them?
Hurry now, tell them—tell Old Wang the Third,
Tell the Eldest Chou and all his eight brothers,
Tell all the farm-hands living round the Lin Huai Gate,

Tell that red-faced ironsmith Lao Li,
Tell One-eyed Dragon and Wizard Hsu,
Tell Old Woman Huang and all the village women,
Tell them all these things, one by one,
And tell them to return, oh, tell them to return!
How strange it all is, and how sad it is!
Heavens, is there nothing to keep people in a fine village like this?
A paradise on earth without a man!

Translated by Ho Yung.

HO CHIH-FANG

Ho CHIH-FANG *inhabits the Gobi desert; he writes (or rather wrote) as easily in the old antithetic style as in the new. He is famous for his essays, the lucidity of his verse and his gentleness. His poems flow like streams, but the streams are deep and often turbulent.*

Born in 1911 in the province of Szechuan, he received a strictly classical education (which still circumscribes his work), and remained with his family until his fifteenth year. In 1931 he entered Peking University, where he studied Chinese philosophy and began to write leisurely. It was the year of Hsu Chih-mo's death and of violence among the students, who opposed the entry of Japan into Manchuria. He took part in the Crescent Society, published a few pieces in the Literary Quarterly *and the* North China Daily, *and in 1936 wrote* The Painted Dream, *which won the literary prize of the* Ta Kung Pao. *When war broke out in the following year, he left Tientsin where he was teaching and returned to his native Szechuan. There he wrote a travel diary called* The Return of the Native, *and later accompanied Pien Chih-lin on his journey among the guerrillas, and returned with a volume called* The New Shansi, *in which the precious artifices of his earlier work had completely evaporated. His collected poems were published in Chungking in 1945.*

THE STREAM

The streams are my companions when I am abroad,
But what are they singing?
My words are as nothing,
Yet I know where there is a desert, there is no water.

You flow beside the little town where we live:
We wash our clothes and feet in this water.
Among the silent hills we hear you
Like the pulse-beat of the earth.

Long have I loved men's songs, and the songs of Nature,
Yet I know where is no sound, there is solitude.

O STORM, O THUNDER

I come from the gloomy tunnel of my world
Into the immense, open universe,
And walk through the habitations of men,
Uncovering their secrets.
I know that men could live in other ways,
And all these ways are contained within his soul.

But when shall these days come?
Days glittering, days sweet, fresh as songs?
O my neighbour, O my brother, O you people in distress—
Let us forge a way into the future, forever searching.
Such days will come at last,
Following unnumbered evils there will come
A great storm, a great thunder.

THE THINGS THAT REMAIN

WHAT things remain?
Is not men's toil in the hot sun in vain?
O you men hurrying from your cradles to your graves!

Sometimes there sounds a voice in my heart
Of an ancient and hideous evil,
Though the voice seems to come from one who is delicate and
    young;
For when I pore over books of history at night
Many a great stone tablet do I see,
And many torches burning in the darkness of Time:
And whether they are held by philosophers or poets,
I can feel their still-beating hearts aflame:
The hearts beating with a wild sound,
Our own hearts beating in harmony with them,
And so we grow larger by little increments.
In the dead of night all is calm.
Only the river flows ceaselessly outside my window.
Now at last the great faith lives within me:
I know that the works of man are the things that remain.
The books I read, my house, all my tools,
And all the things that fill my brain like honey in a honeycomb,
All these are sealed with wisdom and proclaim the labour of
    the ancestors.

THE FABLE

THE mermaid in the fable
Desired, so they say, to become a woman,
And by a fairy's charm, she lost her tail:
Then lived in the world of men.
Soon she learned to speak, saying:

"O men, you are so fair,
With your voices you exchange your thoughts,
You play in the air.
Please do not rebuke my shyness,
Nor my stammering words,
For I am not yet accustomed to this strange world."
Immediately, a man embraced her.
She fled away from him, trembling
Lightly from head to foot:
Then uttered her first laugh
And shed her first tears.
Since then she has always been laughing and shedding tears,
And according to the fable, she has become the sister of men.

LET ME SPEAK OF PURE THINGS

Let me speak of pure things:
My earliest loves, my earliest friends.

The scented flowers on earth, and the stars,
Men—their wild hearts and souls.
Nothing can remain for ever.
All fade like the morning dew.

But what remains is so precious.
Their shining is a hostage to eternity.
Sitting on the grass, reading with my friends,
Walking under the stars, speaking of the future.
The poor children thought us rich beyond dreams.
Then once I loved a girl silently,
And would do anything she demanded of me.
My love was like the moon in all its fulness,
But now Time's ashes have shrouded my heart.

For too long have these things remained silent in my memory:
For a whole age my loves have remained in their tombs.
Now I am no longer young:
Time passes me by.
Yet still there are youths on the earth,
And everywhere the young hearts are opening.
O young comrades, let us go out into the wild lands.
Let us speak of pure things
Under the blue sky—this serenity!

NIGHT SONG I.

Once again wake from dreams!
Open your eyes for daybreak.
Recall the past days to your mind.

Tears fall on the pillow,
And yet there is no sin in tears.
There are tears of joy and of sorrow,
There are tender tears, and tears of glory—
O, you who are so young, merely a boy,
Who have grown up in the adoration of men,
Why do you weep in your sleep?
You say you are on fire,

And the flames are fanned brilliantly,
You say wisdom is pain,
And there is much grief in beauty:
I tell you, there is no wisdom in pain,
And there is beauty in contemplating beauty.

There is no reason for your loneliness:
Everywhere on earth, in the heat and the cold,

We are all gardeners,
Nor can we alter the seasons,
Nor can we make the beautiful more beautiful,
But sometimes we can change them;
We can bring a greater warmth and fragrance to the earth.
O you, who have just begun the race,
Do not say that fortune is frowning on you.
Let us grasp happiness from the earth.
If there is none,
Let us make it from the earth.

Never say, O beginner in the race,
That these things belong to the future.
Those who come after us
Will sport in the sun,
And shall you be jealous:
Since we carry the bright standards,
And to-morrow there is happiness.

Sleep sound during the long, silent night.
Rest: do not brood at night.
Have strength in the morning to welcome the dawn.
Sleep sound: O gently close your eyelids.

NIGHT SONG II.

My mind is like a window breaking open,
My thoughts come in clouds
In this May night.

During the day the sun is too hot;
During the night the moon is too bright.

I cannot rise from my bed and walk in the woods;
I cannot be like Shelley, nor can I be like Ariel
Flying over the fields and valleys.
I cannot sit on the beach, sighing:
"I have neither hope nor health,
Nor fame, nor power, nor love, nor any leisure.
I cannot sing of your love:
I cannot sing:
'*I arise from dreams of thee . . .*'
All day you succumb to your leisure,
And all through the summer nights you lie in the grass,
Sleeping through all cool seasons.

Tell me, Ho Chih-fang, why do you have this hatred of nature?
In your books you have described her well—
Always beautiful, always charming.
But for you nature is no more than an ornament,
And you yourself hold men in greater worth.

We have lost the simplicity of the previous century.
We are the forerunners,
Talking of war.
We must all take our part in this war,
Which is no more than a civil war,
Among simple people
Whom I would embrace with my love.
O, but at last they will awake,
The war will be transformed into something else,
And from the deaths of millions perhaps
There will arise a new world.

Let me talk of Lenin.
I see him touching the heads of children, saying:
"Perhaps there will be a new world,
Perhaps there will be less cruelty."

I see him sitting before the windows in the early morning:
"I am writing to a comrade in the country.
He is lonely, he is tired. I must soothe him.
Because his melancholy is not a little thing."

I hear
His loud, high voice
Shaking the rafters of the Assembly:
"We must dream."

So we must dream,
Continually surpassing ourselves.

HAPPINESS

TELL me, what is happiness?
Is it doves' wings, the red beaks of swallows?
Is it playing on shepherds' pipes,
Is it the babbling of pines and streams?

Is it tender hands which can be held?
Eyes speaking with affection and pity?
Something which makes men's hearts shiver?
As grief does, moving you to silent tears?

Where does it come from?
Is it a glowworm hiding in the shadow of trees?
A fragrance wafted from a rose-petal?
Something which sings with rings on its feet?

O happiness, my heart is like the eyes of a blind man.
I do not see you. Are you as lovely as my melancholy?
Translated by Chiang Shao-yi.

FENG CHIH

HE *looks like the younger Goethe with his courtliness, his immense mane of black hair and his air of grave, unending abstraction. He is devoted to Goethe and Rilke above all, and their influence is visible in his poems; an influence which does not prevent him from understanding the great trends of Chinese philosophy. Rather more than any other poet included here, he has formed a bridge between east and west, and one reads his poems with the sensation that east and west have at last united into a single conspiracy—a conspiracy of beauty and tenderness, and of a childlike grief in tragedy. His images of duckweed, of children and of the vastness of the night come from China, but they are seen through eyes so clearly accustomed to the proportions of the west that we feel no strangeness: the insubstantial bridges acquire form and colour; and we pass over them as easily as we pass down the lanes of our native land.*

Feng Chih was born in 1905 in the province of Hopei. After graduating from Peking University, he studied German literature and philosophy at Heidelberg, having already published two collections of poems: Songs of Yesterday *(1927) and* Northern Wanderings *(1930). There followed a long silence, and it was not until 1941, after the Universities in Peking had traversed the length and breadth of China to find refuge in the ancient city of Kunming, that he began to write again. The Japanese bombardments of Kunming drove him into the country away from books, and it was there that he wrote the twenty-seven sonnets of which fifteen are included here. The sonnets show the influence of Rainer Maria Rilke rather than of Goethe, but those who are acquainted with T'ang poetry will recognise a curious kinship with the old Chinese masters. The form has changed—the quatrains of the past can no longer hold the emotions of the present—but there is the same delicacy which we find in Wang Wei and in the poems which Li Po wrote in retirement from the world. Now Professor of German language and Literature at Lienta, he remains curiously alone as a poet, taking part in no movements and assuming no disguises, a young Goethe going out in search of his inheritance.*

I

We are prepared to accept in our hearts
Those unexpected miracles:
After an eternity of days, suddenly
The comet's appearance, the whirlwind rise.

In those moments of our lives,
As in a first embrace,
Past sorrows and joys before our eyes
Crystallise into solidity.

We, admiring the small insects
Which after a single copulation
Or a single encounter with danger

Terminate quietly their delicious lives,
Knowing that our whole life is a waiting for
A whirlwind's rise, a comet's appearance.

II

Whatever can be shed from our bodies
We allow to turn into dust.
We prepare ourselves for this age
Like the autumn trees which, one by one

Surrender their leaves and late flowers
To the autumn winds, and so offer themselves
Unencumbered to hoary winters: we prepare ourselves
In nature like the cicadas,

Leaving our husks behind us on the earth.
So we prepare ourselves
For our forthcoming death like a song

Shed from the body of music,
Till music herself is left naked,
Transformed into a chain of blue silent hills.

III

OFTEN when I meditate on man's life
I cannot but pray to you,
You—a small bundle of whitish grass,
And yet I do not profane your name.

For you avoid taking any name,
And lead a trivial and humble life.
Claiming neither nobility nor purity
You quietly achieve your birth and death.

All the claims of this world, and its noise
As they come before you, fade into nothing
Or are received into your silence.

This is your great pride,
To be won only by self-denial:
And therefore I pray to you on behalf of man's life.

IV

OFTEN I see in the wild fields
A village boy or a farmer's wife
Who is crying to the unregarding sky.
Is it because of some crime?

Or because of a broken toy?
Or because a husband died?
Or because a son grew sick?
Crying so disconsolately,

As though the whole of their existence
Was enclosed in a frame, and outside
There was no more life or world.

To me it is as though from the world's beginning
These tears have been falling, falling—
For a whole universe in despair.

V

It is an old, old dream:
Since the present world is full of cares,
We wish to soar with the eagles
And talk with the quiet stars.

This dream of a thousand years resembles an old man
Who yearns for the greatest among his offspring—
Though men now fly towards the stars,
Still they cannot forget the world's cares.

And therefore it often happens that in order to learn
How to fall and how to revolve,
Or how to imitate the starry order,

They project themselves into the air like light,
And then the old dream becomes
A meteorite falling into remote wildernesses.

VI. VENICE

I shall never forget
That city lying on water in the West.
It is a symbol of human society,
A congregation of a thousand solitudes.

Every solitude is an island,
From island to island there are bonds of friendship:
When you shake my hand,
You are throwing a bridge over the waters.

When you throw me a smile
A window opens for a moment
In a house on a neighbouring island.

As night deepens and closes,
So, too, do the windows close,
And there are no passengers on the bridges.

VII. GOETHE

You were born to a common burgher's family,
And many a tear you shed for an innocent, humble maid.
You bowed low before the powerful ruler.
For eighty years your life was tranquil.

Like the revolving universe, solitary,
And like the universe moving without pause,
Forever offering new germs of life
In spite of wind or rain or burning sun.

From heavy sickness emerges new health,
From despairing passion emerges new hope.
You also know why the moth seeks fire

And why the snake sheds its skin in order to grow.
For all things obey your legendary phrase—
The secret of life resolved in "death and change".

VIII. VAN GOGH

Your passion brought fire wherever you travelled,
You kindled a bunch of sunkissed yellow flowers
And set fire to a row of sombre yews:
And those walkers under a burning sun,

They also became quivering flames,
Praying and appealing to the heights:
But a small tree in the early springtime,
A prison courtyard,

Men peeling potatoes in a dark room
With their heads bent low, these remained
Frozen in ice, never melting—

And besides these you painted
Drawbridges and elegant boats. Did you intend
To ferry over some of these unfortunate passengers?

IX. TU FU

You starved in deserted villages,
Always you saw ahead of you a gutter death,
And yet you were incessantly singing
Of the glorious events which occur each day.

Warriors died, lay wounded on battlefields,
Stars fell down the sky,
A thousand horses vanished in scudding clouds.
To all these your life was a sacrifice.

Your poverty still glitters and shines
Like the rags of a deceased saint,
And the least tatter which remains

Is endowed with magic powers.
Their crowns and purples in this light
Are shoddy compared with yours.

X. LU HSUN

In the deep night many years ago
You were awakened by our youthful courage.
God knows, you were disillusioned many times,
But in your mind the awakening never faded.

Therefor I shall always be grateful to you,
And gaze up at you on behalf of our age,
Wherein the fools reign untrammelled,
Yet the real nurse of our age was always

An exile from this world.
Sometimes you saw the light come clear through the clouds,
Then—a turn of the head—the clouds came again.

Now you have come to the end of your remorseless journey.
During these trials only the roadside grass
Called forth from you a hopeful smile.

XI

Often we spent an intimate night
In a strange room, and we did not know
How it looked during the day,
And we knew less of its past and its future.

We saw the infinite landscape beyond the window,
And we remembered the dim road
Through which we had come at dusk. That was all we knew.
Departing to-morrow, we shall never return.

Close your eyes! Let those intimate nights
And unfamiliar places be woven into our hearts.
Our life is a landscape beyond the windows,

And there in the descending light we discern
A tree, the glimmer of lake water, infinite visions
Which rise from the forgotten past and the fading future.

XII

In the depths of the night, in the depths of the mountains,
Listening to the melancholy fall of rain,
The village ten miles away, and
The city twenty miles away—

Do they still exist?
These hills and villages visited ten years ago,
And those dreams we enjoyed twenty years ago,
Surely they have all dissolved in the rain!

Everything around us is closing in upon us:
It is as though we were returning into the womb.
O God, I beseech you in the depths of night

Like those ancient men who prayed:
"Give, give to our narrow hearts
A wide, wide universe."

XIII. ON A PUPPY

For half a month it has rained without cease,
And ever since you were born,
You have known nothing but damp and gloom.
Now at last the clouded sky is clear.

The sun shines on the entire face of the wall.
I see your mother
Taking you by the mouth into the sun
So that your whole body

Is soaked for the first time in light and warmth.
When the sun sets, she will take you again
In her mouth. You have no memory:

But all this experience
Will form a part of your future bark.
You will bark forth brightness into the depths of the night.

XIV

For thousands upon thousands of years
This place seems to have spoken aloud
Of our life as it is.
Even before we were born.

There was a singer
Who sang of our fate,
Pouring his songs through the changing sky,
The green grass, the emerald pines.

And we, who are full of cares and sorrows.
How is it that we in this place
Hear such heavenly songs?

Look, the small insect is flying.
Murmuration of wings,
Throbbing with eternal life!

XV

Day after day we follow the familiar pathways
To reach our dwelling-place,
Although in the forests are concealed
Many paths which are deep and obscure.

If we take a strange road, we find ourselves trembling
Lest we go further and further astray:
Until unexpectedly, through a thin veil of trees,
Appears the house, our dwelling-place

Like a new-found island above the horizon.
Many are the things near and round us
Which await our discovery:

Never believe they are all known and familiar to us.
For touching one's own hair and skin when dying
We may yet ask, whose body is this?
Translated by Chu K'an.

PIEN CHIH-LIN

SLIGHT, *and short, wearing spectacles, working alone in a bare room where the only decorations are a few books and a map of the world hung upside down, Pien Chih-lin has the ruthlessness of the old scholars, and their terrible, sweet smiles. To a quite extraordinary degree, he represents all that is best among the younger Chinese poets. He has the solitude, the occasional ferocity, the gentleness and the delicacy of the old poets, and it is not for nothing that he worships Henry James and Mallarmé, the two most Chinese in spirit of all foreign writers. He has not made a bridge like Feng Chih between the two worlds of east and west: he still inhabits the desert of Gobi, that strange land between the frontiers where everything surprises and snow turns into sand. Yet the scholar who looks like a shy student spent two years with the guerrillas in the north-west: the frail body hides unseen powers of endurance.*

He was born in 1910 near the estuary of the Yangtse river, and attaches mysterious significance to the fact. He entered Peking University in 1929, graduating in the summer of 1933, a few days after the publication of his first collection of poems: Leaves of Three Autumns. *Some of these poems had already appeared in the* Crescent Monthly *and* Poetry, *where his fame as a translator was first acquired. In the extraordinary quantity and perfection of his translations from Baudelaire, Verlaine, Mallarmé, Henri de Regnier, Paul Fort, Francis James, Paul Valéry, Jules Supervieille and Paul Eluard, there were signs of a verbal dexterity which would, if they had been continued, compromise his whole life as a poet; and when the Japanese War of 1937 began, he switched suddenly to the simpler and less sophisticated English poets of the present century. He has a disturbing adoration for Auden, and a respect for Yeats and Eliot which approaches divinology.*

For years he contributed to the Literary Quarterly *and* Ta Kung Pao, *but more recently he has been busy editing a vast series of translations from western literature. He has begun a translation of Feng Fei-*

ming's "The Bridge", which may never be completed; he has translated half of André Gide and the whole of Lytton Strachey's Queen Victoria. He wrote a short essay in prose called The Seventy Second Regiment *about his experiences among the guerrillas around the Taihang Mountains in the first year of the war, and is now at work on a vast novel of Chinese life to be called* Those Mountains, Those Waters, *which promises to possess all the delicacy, which he admires in James, and the breadth which comes from a long training in literature and among guerillas.*

His collected poems, composed of four parts, Resounding Dust, Outside the Resounding Dust, Ornaments for Chang Hsuan and Twenty Letters, *were published in 1940.*

PEKING

Peking city: flying kites on a rubbish mound,
here a butterfly, there an eagle
painted on the blue canvas over Madrid.
Across the sea of sky, what a pity that no one can see you,
Kyoto!—

O trailing a trail of dust
and leaving all the passers-by in a showerbath,
flying wheels, you swim in so shallow waters,
yet in so high spirits?

Not so dusty indeed, even *they* are running away
from something hot at their heels, howling over their heads,
over everyone's head. Here it is again:
The yellow-haired wind makes a mess of the immense incense-
    pot,
stirring up the ashes of many centuries,
sending them flying, flying, flying,
driving them into frightened horses, fierce wolves, furious tigers,
rushing, rolling, roaring along the streets,
swooping over your windowpanes, giving you a puff,
swooping upon your ears'-eaves, striking off an ear,
or a glazed tile?—

"Dear me! Simply frightened me! Lucky it isn't
a bomb! Ha, ha, ha, ha!"
"Sweet is it? Enough of your fragrant dream?
No rider in your ricksha, yourself lying there as on a sofa,
Lucky indeed the tile has eyes!"
"The bird's dropping has also eyes—ha, ha, ha, ha!"

Ha, ha, ha, ha, what's the fun of it?
hysteria, you understand, hysteria!

Sad, sad,
really sad to see the child imitating the old man,
young as he is, flying kites on a rubbish mound,
he also hums the threadbare tune "On recalling the Past . . ."
Sad, sad, to hear a city of hoary trees
crying vainly,
crying, crying, crying.
homeward? where? homeward? where?
Ancient capital, ancient capital, what can I do for you?

I am a kite already severed from the string,
having stumbled on you, how could I not cling
on your dear willow-branches? You'll be my home, you'll be
    my tomb;
just send your catkins on every bower, every tower,
never mind if my looks are day by day withering away.
That's rotten, pardon: look here,
Peking city: flying kites on a rubbish mound.
Yesterday the weather was really in a nice mess, wasn't it?
Old Fang complains of Heaven every spring: cursed it yesterday,
Because it crowned the city like an immense yellow tomb.
Old Wang said it looked ominous: if you once dropped asleep,
maybe you would never see daylight any more
until the excavations of your descendants many centuries later.
But to-day the weather is really splendid, isn't it?
See the flowering trees posed on barrows for a spring promenade,
and we'll enjoy lanterns of vermilion silk over the peonies.
(Over there, are they now enjoying their cherry-blossom?)
It's the doves' flutes that whistle in the sky,
blue sky with white doves, no airplanes—

Even the airplanes appreciating the view, I assure you,
would not be so hard-hearted as to lay eggs on these glazed tiles.

Peking city: flying kites on a rubbish mound.

THE COMPOSITION OF DISTANCES

WHEN I dream of reading alone on the highest terrace
"The Decline and Fall of the Roman Empire"
there appeared in the newspaper the star that marks the Fall.
The newspaper drops on the floor. The atlas opens
to a thought travelling to a far-off name.
The landscape received here is now clouded with twilight.
("Waking from a wandering dream to find it is dusk,
listless, shall I go calling on my friend?")
Gray sky. Gray sea. Gray road.
Where have I been? Alas, I can never know
how to examine a handful of soil beneath a lantern.
From outside a thousand doors suddenly comes my name!
How tired! No one really stirred the boat in my basin,
no one caused a storm in the sea?
O my friend has brought me five o'clock
and the sign of impending snow.

THE AQUEOUS ROCK

Pondering on leaving some inscription
on the rock beside the stream, the traveller
pours his feeling into a quiet flow of words:

The boy who admires the charms of the baby
asks his own mother: "Was I like this too?"

The mother, reminded of her own photographs
which have turned yellow in a dust-sealed drawer,

and of the profusion of splendours outside the window
garnered in a frameful of shrivelled pods,

exclaims: "What a seed of sorrow!"

"O water, O water!" sighs the traveller,
startled at the sudden realisation
that wave over wave of ancient emotion
has flowed like the running stream,
leaving behind layer after layer of sorrow.

FRAGMENT

You take in the view from the bridge,
and the sightseer watches you from the balcony.

The gracious moon adorns your window,
and you adorn another's dream.

FIRST LAMP

Birds engulf hard pebbles to grind the grain in their crops.
Beasts fear fire. Men keep fire, and so arises civilisation.
Blessed are those who arise at sunrise and sleep at sunset,
yet I praise the first lamp that opens on a new world.

RESOUNDING DUST

The postman startles the familiar ring of the bell,
startling the heart of the householder.
Is it a fish that comes swimming through the Yellow Sea
or a wild goose hovering after its journey *via Siberia?*
"Open your map," my friend tells me from afar.
The town he shows me is a black point near a dotted line.
Were it a golden grape and my seat the summit of Taishan

on a moonlight night, I would be sure the place you speak of
is just a solitary railroad station.
Yet I have been musing over a book of history,
looking forward over the ancient road to Hsienyang.
I've heard the herald hooves of quickening horses!

SOLITUDE

The country boy, in fear of solitude,
kept a chirping cricket beside his pillow.
Grown up, though toil in the city left him no void,
he purchased a night-illuminating watch.

While a child, he envied the crickets
who took the weedy gravemounds for their gardens.
For three hours he has been dead
and yet the watch continues ticking.

FISH FOSSIL: A FISH OR A GIRL SPEAKING

I want to possess the form of your embrace,
for I'm often melted in the lines of water.
O you who love me like a mirror glass,
When we are both gone, here is formed the fossil.

LATE ON A FESTIVAL NIGHT

The window before the night-light shines like a mirror:
don't lift the curtain, don't gaze deep in the night,
if you don't want to be thrown back upon yourself.
Yet the far-off window is a deeper mirror.
Look at the winking spark of the waking lamp,
whose eye is it that looks so sad?

"A pity that I can't hear with you my sleeping breath!"
is as sharp as a knife, yet it won't slice the whirlpool:
You are the other's dream while the other is in yours.
The lonely riser casts away his chilling knife
and blesses you both.

THE RAIN AND I

"It has rained every day since you left."
"Since you came, it has rained every day."
For the rain over my friends in two places I am responsible.
No news from the third—should I send an umbrella?

Anxiously I gaze through the green grass to far horizons.
Are the birds safe in their nests and men on strange pillows?
Let me place a deep glass in my courtyard to see to-morrow
how many inches it rains to-night in the world.

TEARS

Has the wailing oriole no tears?
Shed them for me on the topmost flower!
                                        L<small>I</small> S<small>HANG-YIN</small>

H<small>EARING</small> the weary steps on the snow outside the door
and the palpitation of the restless fire,
how could one have no tears?
To ask on the land whether on the sky or the sea
there are roads or no roads
carries nowhere yet it has started a longing.
This flight of birds come home from my native place
I should say, for the birds have their home
as the bees have their home,

a tiny shell picked up on the seashore,
a tiny button fallen from an old shirt,
a tiny key of a lost box
have all their home
in my suit-case that accompanies me north and south,
like pearls in the mother-of-pearl.
The walker in the lane and the tree inside the wall
have really nothing to do with each other?
No more than shedding a drop of yesternight's rain
on the shoulders of a dusty coat?
It is not that one has no tears:
only one knows the kinship between the dew and the morning.
Come and draw a tangent.
I will treasure up the point which occupies no space,
like a pearl or a tear—
One may well have tears.

THE MIGRATION OF BIRDS

How many pieces of blue sky after how many courtyards
divide among yourselves? I will go.
Let the white doves with flutes weave three circles around your
    head—
yet await, the camel-bells have gone, do you hear?
Spin the top to encircle you, fly the kites to entangle you,
let the three or four hawks, paper-swallows, paper-cocks
all soar to greet the wild geese from the south?
Am I a toy for children?
Just go to the library, borrow a *Migration of Birds*.
Do you agree, by the way, or oppose the new order
prohibiting the passage of airplanes
through the municipal sky?
My thoughts are like gossamers the small spiders ride
pulling me back only to float me forward, I will go.

Let me consider when I am somewhere else
how many pieces of blue sky for how many courtyards.
How could I pose for ever like a desperate radio
that vainly stretches its arms on the roof
to snatch from afar its desirable waves of sound?

THE PENINSULA

THE peninsula is a slender finger
pointing to the three fairy sea-hills.
The small white house is already surrounded on three sides
with water sweet to the eye, but not to the tongue.
A fountain has then risen in the courtyard:
and lines of footprints have been traced towards the door.
The beckoning diamond you yearned for last night
is to-day the very place that shelters you.
O gather up the waves in window-curtains
lest the guest ponder now those impatient sails.

THE HISTORY OF COMMUNICATIONS AND A RUNNING ACCOUNT

THE mud in a river flown in a bill to your eaves,
the neighbour's fountain flown through a pail to your glass,
jewels from beyond the ocean anchored in your breast:
I want to study the history of communications.

A fleeting sigh paid last night,
a radiant smile received this morning.
Paid: a flower in a mirror. Received: a moon in water . . .
I keep for you a running account.

THE DOORMAT AND THE BLOTTING-PAPER

I TAKE care to scrape my soles on the mat before your door
that I may not spoil your room with dust from the road
in return for your care in covering with blotting-paper
the envelope that its face may not be blurred with tears of
    words.

Imprints of sorrow left on the mat, on the blotting-paper also.
I know that sea-water can cleanse this worldly glitter.
A white kerchief may at least enclose a little coral,
yet you prefer to see it wave on the platform with green flags.

THE GIRL AT THE DRESSING-TABLE

THE world enriches my dressing-table, turning it
into a shop of fruits surrounding me with rosy sweets
all keen to be taken, yet how can I help
if my appetite after the morning dream is so weak?

Gossamer, you ought to have tied yourself to the eaves,
Willow-catkins don't fall into the water of my basin.
Mirror, O naughty mirror, you simply annoy me:
let me draw first two curves of saintly brows on you!

Yet from the joy of each pair of mandarin duck tiles,
I realize the perfection of the roof and appreciate
the *wut'ung* green with distinct leaves of emerald—
Behold the oriole dallying on the twig with her bill!

Shall I not give that new dress a graceful life?
"To adorn means to lose oneself in something else"—
Who wrote these words to me? O, I won't go on recalling—
Odious! "I complete myself to complete you, dear."

NOTES

THE COMPOSITION OF DISTANCES

A news report dated December 25, 1934, recorded that a new star in the constellation of Hercules had been discovered a fortnight earlier by an amateur astronomer in Norfolk. Estimated to be 1,500 light years from the earth, it must have burst into sudden brilliance at the same time as the fall of the Roman Empire.

In P'u Sung-ling's *Strange Stories from a Chinese Studio* there is a story of a magician. One day he left the house, ordering his disciple to watch over a basin covered by another basin, and forbade the disciple to uncover it. When he had gone, the boy opened them and found in the clear water a tiny boat equipped with the masts and sails of a junk. Surprised, he stirred it with his finger and upset it, but after setting it right, he covered the basin as before. When the magician returned, the boy was upbraided for his disobedience. The boy denied all knowledge of the crime, but the magician answered: "My ship on the sea was capsized a moment ago. What is the use of lying to me?"

RESOUNDING DUST

The phrase "resounding dust" is used in literary Chinese for tidings or news, but is here restored to its original associations.

The fish and the wild goose are legendary messengers who carry messages for men, the first in its belly and the second in its foot.

Tai Shan is the sacred mountain on the top of which Confucius is supposed to have sighed over the smallness of the world.

The allusion in the last two lines is to Li Po's famous line: "No more resounding dust along the ancient Hsienyang road." (Hsienyang was once the capital of the Ch'in dynasty.)

FISH FOSSIL

Black characters need white paper. After writing down this little poem of four lines and reading it over, I find that it might well serve as a motto for an album bearing a design of a fish fossil on the cover.

I think of what Paul Eluard says: "She has the shape of my palms. She has the colour of my eyes."

We have the Chinese counterpart in the saying of the classical historian, Ssuma Chien: "Women's looks are for those who are delighted with them."

I think also of Mallarme's mirror, not the famous "O miroir! . . . " in *Herodiade*, but that Venetian glass in *Tremblement d'hiver*, which was "deep as a cool fountain surrounded with gilt banks: what is reflected in it? Oh, I am sure there must have been more than a woman washing away her crimes of beauty in the still water. Perhaps, should I gaze a little longer, I would see a naked phantom".

It is significant that the Chinese engrave on steep cliffs the inscription: "Water flows, the clouds remain."

When a fish has become a fossil, the fish is no longer a fish and the stone is no more the original stone. This is also a sort of death and change. The "I" of to-day is no longer the "I" of yesterday, hence we value "the wild goose's footprints left in the snow", which to the Chinese are souvenirs.

Does the "you" of this poem stand merely for the stone? Does it stand merely for her *him?* Perhaps there is something more. What is it? Let me think it over—no, I won't, for it is already more than enough. (Written at the same time as the poem.)

LATE ON A FESTIVAL NIGHT

This poem was written some eight years ago. Let me now relive the moment recalled by these few lines. Well:.

The night is quiet after all the noisy merriment appropriate to a festival day. It is late. Everybody is back in his or her proper corner, surrendering to a sweet fatigue, perhaps lying by the side of another. Why then do you sit up alone? Writing long letters, as Rainer Maria Rilke says somewhere in a poem? Most likely. At least you must be thinking of someone, for otherwise you would not now lift the window-curtain and look out piercing through the night with your strained eyes. The glowing glass-pane, lined with pitch black, presents to you however an image looking sadly and longingly back at you—your own image! Of course you are not comforted. But come, come, just imagine that the other whom you are thinking of may be performing the same action in some far-off place.

What is distance to the mind's eye? The lighted window, the other one, has drifted at once into your sight from afar like a twinkling spark or better, a drowzy eye blinking and gazing at you. And what is distance to the mind's eye, especially of the lover? You can even make out in the gradually enlarging light a pair of eyes so sad and so full of longing—whose eyes are they? The other's or yours? Yours and the other's? Oh, you can no longer deny that you are quite happy here. You are one, you and the other.

Then what is the use of making the churlish jibe: "A pity that I can't hear with you my sleeping breath!" It might seem well said, bitterly true. Even side by side on a bed, if one of the two falls asleep a little bit earlier than the other, what of the other? Caste beyond, unaccompanied, forlorn, for individuals are at bottom separate cells cut off from one another. But no, this sharp observation can do no harm save perhaps to itself. If even Li Po's all powerful poetic sword fails, as he himself admits, to cut the ever-running water, how could this vulgar knife split apart the whirlpool—"You are the other's dream while the other is in yours." It only proves, on the contrary, the strength of your union to its own cost—most likely to its own salvation by losing itself with the current and then refinding itself flung upon the shore, mellowed with time and rust, to be picked up and to become a new item in the catalogue of a museum or a curiosity shop. Well then, the lonely man who has sat up like you, but who instead of thinking caressingly of another, has given himself over to the infatuated belief that "he is sober alone with all the others drunken", now really wakes to find himself in a frame of mind worthy of a Buddha —a Buddha who has made himself one by following the famous exhortation "Lay down your butcher's knife and you will become a Buddha at once",—and blesses you, you and the other, both.

November 4, 1943.

RAIN AND I

I received a letter from a friend in Shanghai saying: "It has rained every day since you left", and on the same day encountered in Hangshow another friend saying: "Since you came, it has rained every day", as if I were responsible. I was, however, rather delighted with the idea, but soon I thought of another friend in a third place, and I felt quite hopeless before a lot of umbrellas in a shop, for Hangshow is famous for producing umbrellas.

There is in Feng Fei-ming's novel "The Bridge" a remark closely similar to my expression in the last two lines: "No matter how immense might be the rain poured from the heavens, it could never fill up a flower." But here I have laid the emphasis in a different way from Feng: I have derived the suggestion in my poem from the old Chinese saying: "The fall of a single leaf announces autumn all over the world."

Translated by Pien Chih-lin.

YU MIN-CHUAN

Yu Min-chuan, like Feng Chih, has formed a bridge between the eastern and western worlds, and appears to be at ease in both, and in this respect he is perhaps more promising than any other poet included here. He is still young, still vigorous, still open to ideas, and together with his innate courtesy possesses a clarity of mind which is reflected in the white simplicity of his living-room in Yunnan University. Slender and wiry, with immense eyes which brood from behind steel-rimmed spectacles, he resembles a projection of Pien Chih-lin into the future, and one suspects that there is chromium-plated steel in the furniture of his mind, together with the deep-sea fish and the fierce beasts of his imagination. He is modern in the sense that Ai Ching is ancient: there are feelers in his mind that extend far beyond the stars. His poetry is full of reminiscences of Keats, Yeats and Milton, and it is significant that in two lines of a poem which is not included here, he should combine a phrase of Keats with one of his own favourite images:

> *. . . the one whose name is writ in water*
> *has been buried deep in dust.*

Like Pien Chih-lin, whom he admires greatly, he possesses a tortured sharpness of vision which gives him kinship to the great T'ang poets; like Feng Chih he is obsessed with the peculiar relevance for our own time of the philosophers Lao Tzu and Chuangtzu. Wen Yi-tuo once paid him the compliment: "If ever I should write poetry again, I should write like you." As a translator from English to Chinese, he is often superb, for his understanding of the delicacies of the English language is as profound as Pien Chih-lin's, and in the specialist field of translating the ancient classics he has shown an extraordinary acute understanding of the limits and rewards of translation. His translations of the Stone Drums *and of the Ch'ing Dynasty novel,* The Dream of the Red Chamber, *are superb: he threatens to become one of the most important interpreters of the east to the western world.*

He was born in 1915 in the province of Anhui. In 1927, when the revolutionary armies passed through his village, he decided upon a life of scholarship, and has devoted himself to scholarship ever since. In 1939 he graduated from Wuhan University and in 1942, after a brief period of teaching in middle schools, he entered the graduate school of Tsinghua University, where he studied English poetry, retaining at the same time a professorship in Yunnan University. He has since returned to Peiping to take up a professorship at Peking University.

LADY MACBETH

Eleven, twelve, one . . .
black strokes of the clock fluttering and dancing
fluttering and dancing, then falling—
swarming wings of dying moths.

The cloud-eclipsed moonlight night
erects on the window
a tombstone a hundred years old.
Then I came across a revelation—
to be buried in a fish's belly.
Is this the dead solitude of high noon?

A piece of diamond cutting apart an icefield,
the neighbouring baby cries out in nightmare.
So mamma is honey, is wine, is opium.

To look for the affection lost
or to despatch the bewitching image?
Now Lady Macbeth stalks out of her chamber
moves on tiptoe
and with sleeves rolled up
displays her heroism.

WAKING AT THE DEAD HOUR

A thousand cuttlefish are surprised!
Where are the teeth of the crocodile?
He vainly tortures his wide-open eyes
and cannot find even a single salt-sea flower.

Over the brocade bedcloth the thorns are growing.
There are brambles. He turns and turns again.
The heaving pendulum drags time with all its strength.
O miserable brother of earth-bearing Atlas!

WITH A PRECIOUS STONE

WITH a precious stone held in his hand
and a string of pearls hanging from his neck,
the Pagan fondly dreams of ancient Greece.
Wearing a poplar-wreath on his hair
and imitating a cynic,
he goes on pilgrimage, barefoot, to a sacred shrine.

Dante holds a small torch
to guide him as he ascends the winding pass.
The next dawn
at the gate
below a tower longing for sunset
he finds a solemn carving
(Is it Erato?)
alive with warm blood.

THE NIGHT-RAIDING PLANE

BETWEEN Heaven and Earth,
between the planets and the stars,
the green light of the night-raiding plane
intends to seek its final destination
along the orbits of the shooting stars.

From infinite to infinite
the orbits extend for thousands of light-years.

"Thousands?" No—"(x+1)".
Without beginning and without end.
Motion is being.

Copernicus has degraded the earth . . .
When a firefly peers at the heavenly bodies through a reed pipe,
what is the fundamental difference between the sun and a satellite?
Beyond the universe there is another universe,
and after this eternity there is another eternity.

Between the planets and the stars
the green light of the night-raiding plane
bears a shooting star of wisdom.
Our human feet have walked all over the earth,
but only by blind Milton was Eden ever found.

HIGH THE SKY

High the sky and few the stars:
The south-wind creeps with its tendrils
along the lattice of the trellis-window.
So I sit in the bamboo grove alone,
listening to the flute song of the bamboo leaves.

Now the moon creeps up my chair
and I cannot help lamenting for the injured shark
who sinks to the bottom of a mercurial sea
with ten thousand tons weighing down on his breast.

Is it because of wine
or because of my ambition to pursue the roc and leviathan
that I cannot sleep to-night?

Thinking of the paleness of that face,
the sky is suddenly covered with flying sand
and I, too, suffer from a dark affection.

RUSTLING

RUSTLING,
      rustling, rustling,
the fallen leaves bury my thoughts—
no one sweeps them.

Your silent enigma
rolls up my wrecked ship
into a restless sea.

Marvel at the blue sky,
the boundless emptiness,
the empty boundlessness.
Is it the cloud-ascending pilot who drops dead?
Bury your head, please. Study Lao Tzu and Chuangtzu for
    ten years.

HORSES

SMILING and smiling
Darwin eyes these degenerate scions
whose bellies are plastered with their own dung,
whose chests are engraved with the lines of their ribs,
whose foreheads are buried in withered grass:
even the Czar's knout
could not shake their nerves.

Over there bodies are purulent sores
through which the glory of their ancestor flows.
No longer can they remember
how their ancestors, by changing the number
of their toes in primeval caves
irritated leopards and tigers and wolves,
nor how they put on bright satins
to accompany the guitar-playing princess, enjoying the spring,
nor how they bore on their saddles the fierce Mongols
whose bloody tassels
flourished round their white blades, lances and spears,
treading the Highland Pamirs,
pursuing wild winds,
galloping over Eurasia.

Once in history Chao Tzu-an painted them with his brush.[1]
Amen!
A Grecian urn
created eternity out of a moment
by virtue of wax and salt.

One hundred years later they will have humps on their backs.
One hundred years later their posterity will dig up the dreams
 of dinosaurs.

WHY?

Why do you
look ten years younger
with your hair cut and face shaved?
Why do you
seem to have put on your spring costume

[1] Chao Tzu-an, better known as Chao Meng-fu, was a famous painter of horses under the Yuan Dynasty, who received the patronage of Kublai Khan. He died in 1322.

of flying swallow instead of fur?
How can you
open the gates of Heaven
with a key of sesame
and sieze the secret heart of creation?

Ask yourself, please.

Why in one of my eyes
does there hang the portrait of Epicurus
and in the other there lies
the Mermaid Tavern?
Why are all the three thousand Mays lost near the south river,
near my mouth?

THE AUCTION

COMING from different homes,
why are these assembled beauties out of favour?
There bygone days were like Peter Pan's dream.

Those who kissed delicious lips,
those that conspired with women's fingers,
those who tossed in conformity with beeswax bosoms:

those who caught hold of joyful souls
through mysterious round eyes,
those who sucked blood by day and night
by means of ivory suckers,
those who with boundless windy clouds of pines and stones
decorated splendid parlours,
those who bore flame and fatigue in passing over
hundreds of mountains and thousands of waters. . .

Their bygone days were like Peter Pan's dream.
Has Chao-chun[1] still the same affection for the Han Palace?

There—in the Chicago slaughter-house:
hanging on necks of iron wire,
columns of leather,
columns of velvet,
columns of silk
columns of the unnameable things
that bewildered Manet's eyes;
the torsos of fleece and camels' hair
gasoline cosmetics perfumes
bacteria of syphilis
brewed in the city atmosphere.

They have lost the colour of all virgins.
Are they really out of favour, or is it the war
that has thinned out their patrons?
O, listen to the radio above the door:
a gypsy woman calculating destinies.

THE CHILD

THE child sucks his finger before a mirror.
"It is nature," said Kao the philosopher,
"to eat and delight in colour."

Influenced by modern girls, Narcissus
looks proudly at his own image in the water.
"Œdipus complex," nods Freud.

[1] Wang Chao-chun was the famous concubine of the Han Emperor who bestowed her in 33 B.C. on the Khan of the Hsiung-nu as a mark of his imperial favour. Her grave, which remained the only green place in the northern desert, was even more famous than her beauty.

THE TWO EYES

From behind the railing two hungry eyes carved their way,
piercing up into the high blue sky,
and were smashed into powder against the clouds.
The Polar bear dances its clumsy dance,
his universe being only six cubic feet.

Those men and women sauntering in the park,
walking to and fro in the green air,
their fingers peeling oranges,
their eyebrows speaking of love—

Dancing, dancing, the Polar bear
in six cubic feet owns his own universe.
Is it the iron chains or the vulture's beak?
Your irony is like the ever-and-ever—
and-ever-growing liver of Prometheus.
Translated by Yu Min-chuan.

TSENG K'O-CHIA

TSENG K'O-CHIA *is that strange phenomena in modern Chinese poetry, a poet who remains uninfluenced by any foreign movement. Though he was a student of Wen Yi-tuo at Chingtao University, he has retained a complete independence of thought and a vigour of expression which has made him the most popular of the war poets. He has neither Ai Ching's art nor the profundity of Pien Chih-lin. He is entirely unassuming. For a while he was a student at Peking University, where his poems were published by Pien Chih-lin in the* Crescent Monthly, *but no trace of the influence of the Crescent Society can be found in him. The son of a farmer, he joined up at the beginning of the war and writes mostly about the Army, peasants, his abiding love for his native land. Famous for coining new words, he derives his popularity from the fact that he understands the passing moods of the country and writes about them with sympathy and benignity. He is included here because he represents the unchanging tradition of the peasant-poet.*

THE SEA

My country
Is my sea.
I do not deny it. As men say
I have for it a partiality.
I love
Those red hearts,
Those dark faces,
I love
Even the scars on their bodies.
In the high hotels of the city
I cannot sleep,
But in the fragrance of the straw,
In the fragrance of the beanstalk,
In the fragrance of the horses' dung,
On a stretch of bare ground,
I always sleep sound.
Strange?
I ask:
"What child under the son
Does not love his own mother?"

THE NAMELESS STAR

I do not dream
That laurels shall fall about my head.
I only hope
That my lines, like a gale of wind, will blow through all hearts.

You must know
I am a wayward child from the country,
The wide-open country dyed to the colours of seasons,

The country is the cradle of my soul.
Because of the weight of their lives
I have sighed for the peasants:
When their fortune changed,
I shared their joy.
So clever are they when they hold
The hoes in their hands—
A single sweep, avoiding the corn,
Cuts down the weeds.
I admire also
The workman's dexterous axe
Rising and falling
To the rhythm of human energy.

The age stands mighty before me:
Facing it, I grasp my pen.
A fool I would be
If I was afraid of being called an "engineer of the human heart."

I would be a nameless star
Silently glistening in the sky,
Leading the pitch-black firmament
Step by step to a new dawn.

SILENCE

The blue hills utter no sound,
And I also am silent.
Time ceases.
So musing we face each other alone.
I cast down my eyes
To the flowing water,
And the flowing water

Casts up its eyes
To me.
You, red-eyed setting sun,
Please do not betray the mystery!

THE DEAD WATER

THE pool of dead water
Stagnates and moulders.
The sun has burned
On the skin of the water
A number of small blisters.
Men
Come to water their oxen,
And women,
Washing clothes,
Kneel in a row along the shore.
The white geese
Glide on the pool,
Children swim
And dive
And come up again,
This pool of dead water
Is continually laughing
And filled with sunlight.

STILLNESS

THE white dove
Makes circles in the sky.
And thereafter the sky becomes
Immensely broader,

A deeper blue.
A buzzing black fly
Disturbs sleep,
And this midday of June becomes
Longer,
A deeper stillness.

TEARS, SWEAT AND PEARLS

Those bitter tears!
That salt sweat!
Never imagine
They will become pearls for your sons.
Let the evil-smelling sweat
Drop to the earth:
Let them be changed into life-giving grains.
And let tears
Fall into ricebowls,
Then sorrowfully you will drink them.
They will give flavour to your rice!

MIDDAY REST

They put down their work:
Everything they have they put down,
For they want nothing but sleep.
So they sleep.
The earth their bed,
The sun their blanket,
The thin shade of the trees their pillow,
Each man's hand lying on another's chest,
And every hair of their skin
Lifts up its pearl of sweat,

Which glints with a carefree light.
The sun shines through the trees, and dapples
Their tanned skins with a host of white flowers,
And their thunderous snoring
Punctuates the throb of their heart-beats.
Iron wings of sleep enclose their hearts,
And no dreams are permitted to enter
The silence of those who sleep peacefully
In the sleep-filled noontide.
At last they awake and shake themselves,
Filled with new strength.

A GRAVE

A LONG life filled with toil
Encloses him at last.
On the field he once cultivated
Another earth-mound appears.
His grave.
Because his whole life has been
Humble and poor,
There are only a few white grasses waving on top
In the encircling west wind.
When alive,
He often worked on this field.
Now that he is dead, he watches silently
His children working the same field.
When dusk falls,
He will come out of his grave,
To detain a passer-by
And have a quiet talk.

THE FARM

THE yoked oxen
Drive abreast.
One hand holding the plow,
The farmer follows behind.
The fresh earth surges like waves,
Exhaling its fragrance.
With a dog by his side,
The child lies on the ground.
Crows follow the plow,
Slowly flapping wings,
Sometimes alighting on the yoked oxen.

THE RETURN

HE is on leave, he has returned home,
And his family
Are no longer in suspense.
Since he went away
No news came from him,
And with his arrival
There comes the first "homeward letter" they have received.
Now his tongue
Moves like a young stream,
Tinkling, flowing without pause.
His mother sits by the spinning-wheel
As though lost in a dream.
His brother has just left the field
And leans forward, the hoe on his lap.
They are all listening attentively:
Exactly as though a scholar

Were reading them a "homeward-letter".
The children
Shuffle among their elders.
With mingled curiosity, love and fear,
They stretch out their small hands
And touch the revolver hanging from their father's waist.
Meanwhile his wife,
Her face burning,
When no one is looking,
Allows her eyes to run over his body.

RICKSHA-DRIVER

A GUST of wind pierces the tree-tops.
The raindrops fall in front of him, becoming increasingly bigger.
There is only a small, pitiful oil-lamp on his ricksha,
Whose light cannot break through the enclosing darkness.

His mind is as impenetrable as a riddle,
For he pays no attention to the wind and rain.
He remains motionless, a hen drenched in the rain.
The night is long. What is he waiting for?

THERE WILL SOON BE A DAY

THERE will soon be a day
When the earth will change utterly, as a face is washed clean:
A white light will fill the sky,
Despair will be sent fleeing,
Winged men will rise to the height of their dreams,
White doves in a spring gale,
There will be heard the fruitful voices of peace.

O, you still laugh at me
As you laugh at madmen
Who say: "The sun rises in the West,
And the waters of the Yellow River are clear."
But I can prove my words.
When the sun is overcast there are no shadows on earth.
But remember:
"Under the long wings of the dark night,
There broods the white sun."

Translated by Chang Tao.

AI CHING

AI CHING *was born in 1910 in Chekiang, the son of a landowner. After graduating from middle school, he studied medicine for a while, but later went to France against his parents' wishes, where he earned a living by designing Chinese figures for porcelain. Shortly after his return to China in 1932, he was arrested by the police of the French Concession in Shanghai for "harbouring dangerous thoughts" and was not released till October 1935. Thereafter he became a professional writer, often teaching and nearly always editing magazines. Later he journeyed to Yenan, and taught occasionally at Lu Yi Academy, which was founded in honour of Lu Hsun. He is one of the greatest—perhaps the greatest—of living Chinese poets, with an extraordinary capacity for putting the Chinese scene on paper. His greatness lies in his simplicity, his vigour and his majestic love for common things. His vision lies in his simplicity.*

Ai Ching is the child of the poetic revolution begun in 1917 by Dr. Hu Shih, but the original founders of the revolution would not recognise him. He has completely abandoned the old antithetical forms which still remain, thinly disguised, in modern Chinese poetry. Confucius said: "Poetry is teaching." Ai Ching's poetry is essentially propaganda for his beloved north China, its vast unfertile plains and robust men. He refuses to be bound within any given form; the architectonics of Hsu Chih-mo are not for him, and he has stated publicly that the adage: "Cut your coat according to the cloth", means nothing in a rigorous north China winter, where the only possible adage is "Change your coat according to the weather". He has been influenced by Mayakovsky, Verhaeren and Shakespeare—particularly Hamlet, *which he has read many times—but the most lasting influence has been the strange, tortured vision of Van Gogh which he first learned to respect in Arles. And, curiously, there are times when Provence seems to flower in his poetry against the arid soil of north China.*

His published poems include Ta-yen-ho *and* Pei-fang (*Northern Land*), *but he did not achieve fame until the publication in 1940 of* The Man Who Died a Second Time. *Together with Tai Wan-shu he edited a magazine known as* Ting Tien (*The Culminating Point*), *and he has since worked on many other literary periodicals published from Yenan and Kalgan, where he lived till the fall of Kalgan in November 1946. He was one of the leaders under the Chinese Communists of the prodigious output of poetry which occurred all over the Communist areas, and it was largely due to his encouragement that Tien Chien has leapt into fame.*

THE MAN WHO DIED A SECOND TIME

I. *The Stretcher*

When he awoke
He did not know he was still alive.
He had been sleeping on a stretcher:
The soldiers carried him,
And they did not speak.

The weather was frozen in the cold wind.
The clouds sank low and moved swiftly.
Speechless, the wind shook the boughs.
Swiftly, swiftly they carried the stretcher
Through the winter forest.

He had passed through the flames of pain
And his heart was now in such tranquillity
That it resembled a battlefield when the fighting is over:
As tranquil as that.

But still the blood
Flowed from the wound in the soggy bandage,
Drip by drip,
Falling on the winter roads of China.

And on this same night
A solemn procession, ten times larger than before,
Moved up to battle,
Their thousands of feet
Rubbing away the remaining stains of his blood.

II. *The Hospital*

Where were our guns?
Where were our clothes with the bloody stains?
Other soldiers were wearing our helmets.
We wore cotton clothes embroidered with red crosses,
And we lay down,
And there were a thousand other pieces of flesh
Corroded by metallic spirits and by poison gas.
We all of us looked through eyes stained dark with fear,
Suspicious, continually groaning.
The days passed, the days passed.
Each day was a procession of black coffins.
In such a place
The pain of each one
Was no less than another's.
With the only lives we ever possessed
We held back the enemy's advance,
We met their fierce fire,
We shed our blood
For the sake of the place we were guarding.
To-day, lying in bed, lying down,
They said to us: It is all to your honour.
We had no need of honour.
We were ill, and we remembered the battlefield:
And this place was more familiar to us than our childhood homes.
And we were proud of our fierce running
Into the hot flames of guns,
But to-day we are shackled beasts
Chained to iron bedsteads.
We wait, we wait.
Will there ever be an end?

III. *The Hand*

At a certain hour each day
The nurse comes in white cap and white coat,
Silently coming in and going out.
She unwinds the bandages
And softly pulls the cotton-wool from our sores,
And washes away the festering scabs and the blood.
Her thin fingers are more skilful
Than the fingers of our wives,
And even our sisters are not like her
As she washes the scabs and the blood away and dresses our
    wounds.
So, skilfully using her ten fingers,
Those thin white fingers
On one of which a gold light shines—
A gold light flaming above our wounds
Into the corners of our unwounded hearts.
Silently she goes on her way.
Then I look at my hand,
A hand which has laboured with the hoe and held a gun,
Coarsened by incessant labour, and awkward,
Now lying strengthless against my chest—
O hand stretching out from a wounded arm,
I behold you, and her hand also.
I ponder deeply, disturbed in my thoughts,
Deep in thought, I ponder
The fate
That brought those two hands together.

IV. *Convalescence*

Time passed in emptiness.
He left the hospital
Like a prisoner leaving jail.
He had taken off his clumsy cotton coat,
Wore a uniform of thin grey cloth,
The front lapel embroidered with a red cross.
O freedom! the sun! the world! the running Spring!
The multitudes of people in the street made him feel
A strangeness and a great sympathy.
The sun shone on the street.
Life woke with a start from interminable sleep,
Joyful in splendour
The people ran down the street.
Oh, but he was so tired, so tired—
Nobody had yet seen him:
This wounded soldier whose wounds had healed.
To-day he was happy
And very seriously he perceived
His healing concealed a still deeper meaning.
It was only then he felt for the first time
He was himself a soldier,
And like a soldier must be wounded,
And then when he is healed, he must go to war again.
He meditated as he walked,
Pondering his unnatural gait
And his sick face:
Men passed, but no one ever saw
The cloud of pain on his face.
Only the sun, from its high zenith,
Stretched down glittering fingers
To console his pale yellow face,
The face which smiled so sadly . . .

V. *The Walk*

He threw off his grey clothes embroidered with a red cross,
He opened his coat wide, he let the sleeves hang down:
On the broad and straight street of the city he wandered at
　　night,
In an intoxicating immense street continually wandering:
Glamorous sounds everywhere, voices of crowds,
Sounds of wheels, bugles, whistles,
Pressing him, pushing him, spurring him onward
Over level pathways,
Under dazzling electric lights,
On smooth, slippery asphalt roads,
Among processions of glittering sedan-chairs,
Among charmingly dressed girls,
How shabby he seemed,
But suddenly he appeared to broaden his steps
(Wearing the garment of honour),
And there came to his mind the feeling
That it was thus men should walk in the world,
And all men like him
Should walk in the same way through the world.

Oh, he was conscious of his steps,
Lifting up his head, wearing his uniform, striding onward,
All men's eyes concentrated on his bearing,
The face of a warrior in electric light
Was now ashamed
And bitterly afraid of the people
Who knew the secret buried deep in his heart:
And the people paid no attention to him at all!

VI. *The Battlefield*

On a sunlit day
He returned to the battlefield
As though someone had summoned him.

His feet trod
The warm soft causeway over the ricefield.
Oh, this was a sensation of unspeakable delight!
He took off his shoes,
Let his feet soak in shallow ditch-water,
The flowing water drooled through his hands.
So much time had passed
Since he was in the army and wore the badge of the army—
And for the rest of his life now
He would wear this badge:
But to-day once again in the battlefield
(Perhaps for the last time)
He must search for the thing that summoned him,
A thing whose name was unknown.
There was the ricefield swilling with water,
There was the farmer,
There was the buffalo—
All these things were known to him,
All these things were the same.
They said: This is China,
The trees are green, the grasses point to Heaven,
Here there are muddy walls,
Over there are the tile-roofed houses, men walking.
He remembered: People say this is China.
He was walking, walking . . .
What kind of day are we living in?
Stupid day, happy day . . .
Not even on New Year's Day had he been as happy as this!
The world shining silver,

Glittering.
So he smiled at the farmer,
And the farmer did not notice his smile.

VII. *The Glance*

In the deep purple shadows he walked
Along a road stretching out beyond the city,
Avoiding the sunlight, walking in shade,
Seeing carriages rolling past,
Young boys and girls
In neat clothes,
Hearing the laughter in their mouths,
Their speech making him uneasy,
Walking, walking, like a weak and weary old man,
Slowly arriving before the gates of the park,
And there at the gates,
At the foot of the marble archway
Lay the wounded soldier.
Oh, how his heart was startled!
The wounded soldier, perhaps
Had been braver than the others, perhaps
Had wished to die on the battlefield,
But now he could only lie down and groan,
Groan and lie down, groan,
So passing the remaining years of his life.
Alas, who could dare to endure the sight.
To see the man you would burn with hatred!
Oh, let us join in war again!
Let us die happily in the war!
Let us not return maimed!
Let us not cry out before the onlookers!
Nor stretch out dirty and hungry hands
To beg for sympathy!

VIII. *Changing Uniform*

Away with the uniform of grey cloth embroidered with the red
    cross!
Now he wears the green clothes he had worn before,
The blood-stains disappeared,
The bullet-holes patched up.
Wearing them, his heart was like a fountain of emotion
Which made him sink deeper and heavier in his first enlistment:
Yet he seemed to feel an everlasting and indivisible chain
Binding him, binding the uniform to the hospital dress.
He would wear them forever, and in turns.
Yes, in turns. For this is proper
To a soldier. Before the end of the war
For the liberation of China,
These two uniforms would float like hammers,
Banners flung violently
Over the earth of oppressed China.

IX. *Farewell*

They marched away to the sound of fire-crackers,
They marched away to the trumpets which stirred up the dust
    in the road,
They marched away to the voices of the crowds who lined the
    streets—
Let us march along the road of human desires,
Let us march along the road of "today" and "tomorrow",
Let us march along the road of the gratitude of those unborn,
Hearts braced high,
Steps like a single step,
Through walls of people,
Doing away with self-love and pride,

Thinking only of honour,
Knowing only honour,
Pursuing her, gladly dying for her.

X. *The Gleam of the Spirit*

Did you ever know
The meaning of death?
—Live and then die?
The insects and green plants
Go through their transformations,
But how can you imagine it?
The word "soldier" of course
Means—to give one's life in the war,
Dying on river-bank,
Dying in wild lands!
The cold dews will freeze our hearts,
Our dead bodies will decay among duckweed.
Many, many years
Men have employed their lives
Making fat the land,
Also using the land
To feed their lives.
Who can avoid the laws of nature?
—So we die.
Is anything wrong?
Is it wrong to hold a gun on your shoulder?
Staggering in long columns?
Do you ever in your heart
Worry about this thing which is more deep than love?
And when you march to the battlefield,
Do you not always feel:
"I have lived once,
Now I must die."

DIE
So that those unborn
Shall live happier lives than ours?
Glory,
Praise,
Can have no meaning
Unless we are conscious of dying
Of our own will—
This will, which is also
The strong-walled will of the nation.

XI. *Marching*

Heigh-ho, then, march forward, have courage!
Soldiers, fix bayonets!
Bind your multitudinous hearts
Into the single will!
We fight for the freedom of China.
Is there anything to fear?
When we have learned to die with honour?
Heigh-ho, march forward, have courage!
Into the thick of the flames,
Into the trench of bullets flowering!
Look, the enemy trembles
At sight of our strong onward steps!
Heigh-ho, march forward, have courage!
It is time to end
This humiliation, this shame.
From the enemy's hands we must take back
The fate of China.
Could this holy war only
Bring back freedom and happiness . . .
Heigh-ho, march forward, have courage!

The days of glory
Are in our hands!
In unyielding fight
Our lives
Rise: march forward!
Soldiers, fix bayonets!
Heigh-ho, march forward, have courage!

XII. *Falling*

With speed
Like the enquiring flight of lightning,
Without a moment's thought
The flame-like bullet
In a split second, and for the last time
Pierced through his body,
Through his life,
Which had once been returned to life,
And now falls
A tree hewn with a large axe.

Before those eye-windows closed
From which he looked out upon the world,
Before those eyes veiled with ecstatic tears
He remembered
Nothing at all, remembering
No mother who had died,
No girl who had been kind to him.
Simple as that.

A soldier,
Who knew little:
That little: only that he should die
For the war of freedom.

Falling,
He knew only
The earth where he slept was China,
And this only
Because those who knew better
Had told him.

Soon enough
His fellow-soldiers came to search for him:
The last visit paid to him in his life:
But this time
They brought no stretcher,
Only a short-handled spade.
There was, of course,
No choice.
Here, in the earth he had guarded with his life,
Here, on the river-bank,
Here: a shallow grave.

Earth mingled with spring grasses
Covered him,
So that he left only one of all those innumerable pitiful graves
Which stretch like stars over the waste land.
No name
Was marked on his grave.
What use is a name
On a soldier's grave?

SNOW FALLS ON CHINA

Snow falls on the Chinese land;
Cold blockades China . . .

The winds like melancholy old women,
Closely follow one another,

They stretch out cold claws,
Tug at clothes,
Their words are as old as the land,
Murmuring, never ceasing.

Coming out of the forest
And driving a cart,
You O Chinese farmer,
Wearing a fur cap,
Plunging recklessly in the snow,
Where are you going?

The truth is
I am a descendant of farmers.
From your faces
Etched with pain,
I know so perfectly
How people live in the plains,
Passing hard days.

Nor am I
Happier than you.
—Lying in the river of Time
Amid waves of suffering
Which entirely overwhelm me—
Wandering and prison

Have robbed me of the most precious part of my youth.
My life
Like yours
Is haggard.

Snow falls on the Chinese land;
Cold blockades China . . .

Along the rivers of a snowy night
The small oil-flame moves slowly.
In that worn-out black-sailed boat
Facing the lamp and hanging your head,
You sit. Who are you?

O you
Snot-haired and dirty-faced young woman,
Is this
Your house
—a warm and happy nest—
Burnt out by the enemy?
On such a night as this
You have lost your husband's protection,
And in peril of death
You tremble under the enemy's bayonets.

Aiee, on so cold a night
Numerous
Old mothers
Wriggle away from their homes,
Like strangers
Who do not know where to-morrow's wheels
Will take them.
—And
The Chinese road
Is rugged,
Muddy.

Snow falls on the Chinese land;
Cold blockades China. . . .

Throughout the plains on a snowy night
Are lands bitten by war.
Numerous men of tillage

Have lost their animals,
Have lost their fat lands,
And now lie crowded
In hopeless lanes.

The hungry good earth
Looks up at the dim sky
And stretches out trembling hands
For help.

Pain and suffering of China;
Wild and long as the snowy night.

O China,
On this lampless night
Can my weak lines
Give you a little warmth?

THE WINTER FOREST

I LOVE to pass through the winter forest.
No sunshine falls on the forest in winter.
In the winter forest only the dry wind blows
And snow falls on the winter forest.

Winter is lovely in no colour.
Winter is lovely for no birds sing.
In the winter forest a solitary walk is happiness.
I will be like a hunter, lightly passing over,
Nor do I think I will gain anything.

DESOLATION

There are no trees on the mountain,
There are no herbs on the ground,
There is no water in the rivers,
The people have no tears.

THE LAND REVIVED

O let these decayed days
Long ago submerged at the bottom of a river
Be washed clean
And without stain!

On the river banks
Where the footsteps of spring are approaching,
Flowers and grasses grow,
And from the forest
There come
The high and haughty songs
Of the spring birds.

O men of the Spring sowing,
It must be time to sow.
In reward for our labour
The good earth will conceive
Golden grain.

And now—at this moment,
You, the sad poet,
Should do away with your ancient melancholy:

Let hope awaken in your heart
Wounded so long,
For now in this beautiful land of ours
Under the bright sky
Reviving
—Sufferings have gone the way of memory.
Into this warm breast
Will come the new flood
Of the warrior's heart-blood.

THE WORDS OF THE SUN

Open your windows!
Open your doors!
Let me come in, let me come in—
Into your cottages.

I carry the golden blossoms of flowers,
I carry the odours of the forest,
I carry the warmth of sunlight
And the fresh dews are on my body and mouth.

Quick, quick, arise!
Rise your heads above pillows,
Open your eyes under eyelids,
Let your eyes see me coming!

Let your hearts be like small wooden houses:
Open the long-closed windows!
Let me scatter flowers, odours and light,
Warmth and sweet dews into the room of your heart!

INVOCATION TO THE DAWN

A Colloquy between the Sun and the Poet

O POET, arise,
That you may invoke my blessings!

Tell them,
What they have long wanted is about to come!

Tell them,
I come treading the dew by the light of the last star.

I come from the east
Amid the rushing waves of the sea.

Tell the village women to open their hen-coops,
Tell the farmers to lead the cows from their byres.

I borrow your lovely mouth to speak with them:
Tell them I come over the edge of mountain and forest.

Tell them to sweep their courtyards,
And all those places which have been left unclean.

Wake the hard-working women,
O wake the snorers!

Tell the young lovers to rise,
And speak, too, to those who love sleep!

Wake the tired mothers,
The babies lying beside them.

Wake everyone—
Wake up those who are sick and those who are pregnant,

And the old men,
And the people who groan in their beds,

And the wounded soldiers fighting for justice,
And the refugees who have lost their homes and who are now
    wandering.

Wake the unhappy:
I will give them rest.

Wake those who love life:
Workers, mechanics, painters.

Tell the singers to welcome me with songs,
Let their voices be filled with the dews and the grasses.

Tell the dancers to welcome me with their dances,
Wearing only garments of white mist.

O wake all healthy and beautiful women:
Tell them to open wide their doors and windows.

O you, who are a Poet, faithful to your time,
Bring glad tidings to the people.

Tell them to welcome me and prepare:
For at the last crowing of the cock I shall return.

NORTH CHINA

Yes,
North China is sad.
Coming from Sai-huai
A wind bearing sands of the desert,
Blowing away the green life of the north

And the splendour of the sun.
—Dim sweep of greys and yellows,
Thick covering of sand-fog,
Roaring sound in our ears,
Horizon coming closer in terror,
Crazily
Sweeping up the good earth.
Wild desolate fields
Frozen in December's cold wind.
Here are villages and hills,
Here are rivers
Worn—worn out, and the wild graves
Covered with mournful yellow soil.
The lonely wanderer
Stoops and hides his face in his hands
Against the sand and the wind,
Choking,
Staggering forward . . .

Oh, and the asses
With their sad eyes and weary ears
Carry their burdens of earth
And wearily their faltering steps
Move over our long, solitary roads . . .
Long ago the creeks were dried up.
The beds of the rivers show the marks of chariot wheels.
Now the land and people of North China
Sigh for the coming spring,
For the moistness, for the new life.
Only the withered forests.
Only the small houses.
So few. So sad.
Scattered under the grey pavilion of the sky,
The sun invisible:
Here and there groups of wild geese

Flapping their black wings
Crying in misery,
Escaping to the green land,
    the green land of south China.

North China is sad.
Thousands of miles of the Yellow River
Coiling among muddy waves
Through sufferings, through misfortunes.
For thousands of years
The wind and the frost
Have engraved on our northern land
The features of poverty and hunger.
While I, the traveller from the south,
Loving this sad country,
The wind and sand blowing against my face,
The coldness choking my bones—
Never do I curse:
For I love this sad country,
This endless wilderness
Which I worship with all my heart.

I see my ancestors
Leading their sheep, blowing their horns,
Sinking in the evening of this great desert,
Under our feet
In the old loose soft yellow soil
The bones of our ancestors are buried.
—This land was reclaimed by them.
Centuries ago they were here,
Fighting against the powers of nature,
Defending their country,
Never yielding:
They who are dead
Have given us this land—

I love this sad country,
So wide it is, so thin the topsoil,
A country which offers to me its simple language,
Its sweet gestures.
And I believe that this language and these gestures
Will never die:
They will be handed down forever,
    this country
    this land
which is so ancient and so hard-working,
and therefore I love her.

Translated by Ho Chih-yuan.

TIEN CHIEN

TIEN CHIEN *is the unruly symbol of the war, a poet who refuses to obey any rules and who openly defies the ancient traditions of Chinese poetry, only to find that he writes a poetry which is sometimes almost indistinguishable from the* Book of Songs. *There is a simplicity in his poetry which shows no sign of affectation, and in a famous essay Wen Yi-tuo has justly described him as the "drummer of a new age". He uses words like hammer-blows, or simply sets them on a page and listens to them singing. He is capable of whipping himself into a rage and shouting like a dervish, stamping his feet—you can hear the dulled echo of his hoof-beats in the northern sand; and then suddenly, as a cloud vanishes, you see the serene bird in his cage and hear the singing. He is a phenomenon, and more than any other poet here may have changed the course of Chinese poetry, or at least reasserted its ancient simplicity.*

He was born in 1914 near Wuhu (Anhui), the son of a landlord, and published his first two collections, It Is Not Yet Dawn *and* Chinese Ballads *in 1936, finding at first greater acclaim in Japan than in China, where his innovations were apt to be regarded as the impudence unproper in one so young, for his first poems were written when he was barely seventeen in the tortured years which witnessed the attack on Manchuria. The thirty-nine poems included in* It Is Not Yet Dawn *were, however, already mature; they had the stocky virility of a poet who knows in which direction he is running, and he was already experimenting with the hammer-beat poetry, which was to bring him fame. He is free of traditions, though there are times when it appears inevitable that he has read Mayakovsky. He is untranslateable, and the versions given here are further from the originals than most of the others. His poetry is meant to be declaimed—with a violence and a savagery which resembles that of a wild beast, or with a pure singing voice as of the fluted doves in Peking. In 1941 his manner changed: it became less violent and possessed a deeper sympathy for the common courage of the people, and in such poems as* One Gun and One Chang-I, More, The Land is Laughing for You, *and the strange epyllion,* She, Too, Wants to Kill a Man, *it acquires a profundity which it never possessed before. He is the herald of a new age, and as such accepted by an overwhelming majority of young students, but whether there can be much advance on a deliberately simple method remains to be seen. The short introduction to his poems by Wen Yi-tuo has been included here as an appendix.*

IN THE MORNING WE ARE TRAINING

"Awake, awake!"
Every morning the comrade cries
With his whistle.

The sky in
April is
blue.

The Northern
Gardens are
blue.

——in the blue morning, in the blue world, in the blue war.

In the morning
we are training.

ONE GUN, ONE CHANG-I

"The weather colder,
The battle fiercer."
    —said by the fighter Chang-I.

O, THE snow falling!

And the gun
From the snow
Was shooting,
Shooting . . .

So beautiful,
so joyful!

Even your red nose
doesn't snivel.

Your blood is hot,
you are really fighting,
strong,
joyful.

The weather colder,
the fighting fiercer:
Ha!
     Stronger

Who was the first
to shoot?
       Chang-I.
The native of central Hopei.

With his heavy cotton gown
turned inside out,
our Chang-I
looked out over the front.

Chang-I
kept whispering
while holding the gun:
"I come from Chin Cha-yi."

The enemy
came nearer,
nearly ten metres nearer,

And no one minded.
     O the snow was falling!

Bullets
Like snowflakes
Over the hills,
Over the plains.

Chang-I and his companions
Kept fighting steadily,
Steadily
Shooting down the enemy.

Our commander
Attempted to encircle the enemy,
And so ordered
Our forces to retreat.

We withdrew.
    Chang-I with his gun
    Lay in the snow.

Ha!
He was covered with snow.
The enemy
Passed over his body.

One gun
And one Chang-I.
Hao!
Hao!

The gun
From the snow
Was again shooting,
Shooting . . .

THE BLACK HORSE, THE PISTOL AND THE SONG

The black horse,
The pistol,
The song. . . .

Here in China we are walking,
Bearing China's fate
And the misfortunes
Of a whole nation.

We have walked
Thousands of *li*
Like the prophets
Who once carried
The Cross.

Here in China we are walking . . .

FREEDOM IS COMING TOWARDS YOU

We must fight for
This grief-stricken nation.
September lies
Outside the window.
All Asia's fields,
O Freedom! . . .
From this earth of blood,
From this earth of my brothers dead,
Freedom is coming towards us,
Like a wave,
Like a great sea-wave!

I HAVE ONLY A DRAFT OF PAPER AND SOME STAINS OF BLOOD

I, AMONG all my comrades,
have only a draft of paper
and some stains of blood . . .

In camp,
in the evening,
when the candlelight burns my youthful soul,
I rub my hot breast
and silently cry.

THE LAND IS LAUGHING FOR YOU

THIS land
is still living.

(And it is living very well
considering . . .)

In these limitless
hollows formed by mountains our horses
are running,
hooves thumping.

                Ha, the brave slogans!

For you see,
this land is laughing for you!

SONG OF THE MOUNTAINS

The sun shines its torch
Over the mountain.
We are gathering cotton.

Gathering cotton—
Hungry,
Tired:
At evening we return.

The cotton is gathered from the mountain,
We have worked hard,
Like cows and horses.

Do not be afraid.
Let the wind blow,
Let the rain fall.
Afterwards,
It will be our world!

WE ARE FOREVER YOUNG—

The young fire
Burns our young hearts—
We are forever young !

In our laughter
Is health.
In our two blood-coloured hands
Is courage!

MORE THAN ONE HUNDRED

The hearts of the farmers
Are marching on
Like stars of fire!

Their felt hats
Are pulled over their eyes,
Because
The fighting has not yet begun.

Their lances
Are raised
Like flags,
Meanwhile
Women and children
Accompany them.

        "Do not be afraid of being burned!
        Do not be afraid of being killed!
        We are searching for a way
        Of life!"

There,
Far in the distance
More than a hundred farmers
Are coming.

They walk together,
They swing together,
They cry together,
They are hoops of iron.

The snow falls and stops,
And the children scabble in the snow,
Raise it to their mouths.

DOWN WITH THE ENEMY!

MORE than a hundred
Push away the snow,
Push away the blood-stains,
And begin to sing.

So they sing,
Fighting against the enemy,
Cultivating this desert.

THE PEOPLE'S DANCE[1]

ON New Year's Day, 1938, when the Japanese were celebrating their "victory", a Chinese guerrilla danced this dance outside the West Gate. They were watched by the Japanese guards, who were later killed by the guerrillas, and the guerrillas returned to their hiding-places with their hands wet with Japanese blood. No, I cannot imagine this scene, which seems sacred to me, but I hope that in my lifetime I shall see such a scene.

In April, in Sian, we performed the People's Dance. The dance was of the simplest kind, and chiefly concerned the necessity of co-operation among the Chinese. The characters were workers, farmers, students, merchants, Japanese soldiers and traitors.

I dedicate this poem to the memory of the guerrillas of Peiping.

Sian, April 1938.

[1] It is impossible to translate this poem adequately: the phonetic character of Chinese words allows the poet a far greater power of musical suggestion in Chinese than it does in English. The sound of the first six lines in Chinese is roughly: *i go / i go / tsa tsa di / ch'u ch'ang / tyao yao / tyao yao*. The poem has been slightly abbreviated in translation.

One by one
By one
Tsa tsa
We dance.

O we leap!
O we jump!

We are
Neither rebels
Rebelling,
Nor traitors
Selling their country,
Nor old women
Kneeling to the earth
Asking God
For blessings . . .

One by one
By one
Tsa tsa
We dance.

O we leap!
O we jump!

The sounds we make
Are not those
Of merchants
Talking in inns,
Nor of farmers
In the fields,
Nor of reeds
In the wind,
Nor of babies crying . . .

One by one
By one
Tsa tsa
We dance.

O we leap,
O we jump!

Old Kuei
Leads
The dancing
Farmers
And workers.
Look, their thick white faces
Look, their dark black eyes!

You see
Their
Vengeful
Power,
Their
Vengeful
Blood,
Their
Vengeful
Songs.
Fists are clasped!

Fists are clasped!
They want
To branch out
In thousands,
Loudly,
——Together.

Many thousands!
Da! Da!
——Together.

Twining,
Dancing . . .

Projecting
Bones,
Gutted
Flesh
Carries the weight
Of the nation's
Madness
And the nation's
Roaring!

Brave!
Strong!

They stretch out their arms,
To break the chains, to seek after freedom,
The savage chains . . .

Stretching out their arms
Round the necks of traitors . . .

Singing together:
   DOWN WITH THE JAPANESE

"We want to live
At peace in our factories,
In our camps, in our classrooms.
Who can hinder us?

Ah
Singing!
Ah
Dancing!
Ah
Sticks!
Ah
Swords!
Ah
Hoes!
Ah
Guns!
Ah
People![1]

Striking . . .
Marching . . .

Red-brown
Sticks,
Blue-black
Guns,
Yellow
Hoes,
Shining
Swords . . .
    All are raised aloft, all clang together . . .

(*Now in this chaos, in the evening of our fight for freedom, the sound of people's footsteps, the sound of the people . . .*)

---

[1] This song is repeated twice in the original. The extraordinary drum-like and evocative effect of this song can be seen from a rough transliteration of the original:

The black curtain
Is pulled down,
But never will the voice of the people
Be hidden.

*Ah
Kerch'ang!
Ah
Wuyang!
Ah
Bangtse!
Ah
Chutao!
Ah
Chiang!
Ah
Ren-ming!
Ah
Taotse!*

SHE TOO WANTS TO KILL A MAN

**Who
Killed
My child?**

**Who
Killed
My child?**

She cries
She laughs
She sobs:

The robbers came
They pawed me
They beat me with guns
Their swords
Held me from running away
        then
They struck me
Pressed me down . . .

My heart burns
O night of the plain
O roads over the plain
Dishevelled hair
Loosely flowing
Small nose
Tipped to the sky
Small teeth snapping,
Speaking in Shansi dialect:
Get away!
Get away!
Who wants you?
Beasts without shame!
Now she unbuttons the greatcoat
Unwinds
The bloody breastbands
With bent fingers
Touches
Wounded
Nipples
Bleeding
Breast
Rough
Flesh
Strong
Flesh

Filled with shame.
Meanwhile
Her voice
Shooting out
Like heat
On this May night
Shining
On the northern plains:
The farmers
Coming from the earth
Digging up
Buried guns
Polishing them
Filling them with powder
Listen,
Then kill their sheep,
Drink up their wine,
Speak roughly
Saying:
The robbers will come.
Better go.
Pile up wheat-baskets,
Take children,
Leave the village behind.

But on this May night
She laughs
She cries
Where are you going, Po-liang with your bleeding hands?
Let every grain
Of sand
Leap
In a flash of lightning:
I, too, must kill a man!
Never had she killed a man,

Never had she killed an ant.
If a dog
Or a horse
Were beaten cruelly
She would run to the master
Protesting
"The whip must be put down!"
Or if a child
Was hurt and hungry
On the road
She would kiss it
Lick up its tears
With her tongue
Feed its thin mouth
From her nipples
Smile comfort it
Till the day
When the Japanese came
And killed her child
She had never killed a man.

My heart burns!
Like a strong wind
My eyeballs shine
Upon these robbers
Speak Japanese
Si-lu-hua-la[1]
Click-clack of pistols
From leather belts
As they set fire
To her walls
Her own doors

[1] Chinese imitation of Japanese sounds, without any particular meaning.

Her own furnace
Her own bucket
    (every morning she took the bucket to the salt-well)
Her own stove
    (every noon she toasted wheat-cakes on the stove)
Her own donkey
    (every evening she rode to market through mud
        and sand)
Even her head-dress
Even her embroidered shoes
The garments sewn for the child
The wood cradle
Cotton gathered from the hills
All the food:
The yams
The red dates
The vermicelli
ALL BURNED
And her child burned
And
Her
Child
Burned
IN THE FIRE
Small hands waving
Small head turning
IN THE FIRE
CONTINUALLY BURNING

Now
She holds a sword
Against her bared belly
Brandishes it
Swears by it
Says

It leads me
It will take me to them.

>   (Some say
>   While the fire was burning
>   Po-liang took the sword
>   From a place near the window
>   Then crept to the hills
>   Sat on a monk's tomb
>   The sword at her throat
>   Then suddenly laughed
>   Useless to die
>   BETTER TO KILL)

She does not fear
Death
Because she understands
Shame.

SHAME
REVENGE

When
She
Vengefully
Lifts
The sword
She cries
>   —Life and death running along the edge of the swordblade.

"Come, follow me,
Follow me,
O sword,
O sword"

She blesses
The sword,
She swears by
The sword
O the night of the plain
O the road of the plain
On this night of May
In this furnace fire of battle
In confused pain
In mingled revenge
Marching through the night
Blood fanning the flames
They see
The dark plain.

Sound of iron bells
Shining wind
Pulling them together
Like iron chains
Peasants riding to battle
Manes
Uplifted
Breasts of horses
Like bellows
Snow-white foam
Trickling from mouths
Falling on sands
Pulling at reins
Tightly
Calloused hands
Whipping
Whipping
Till at last
Suddenly, slowly
They are afraid

They call out:
"Death is upon us!"
"They will surely revenge—"
"Aiyee! Aiyee! Aiyee!"
"Where shall we go?"
"Where shall we hide ourselves?"

Suddenly, slowly
Hearing a strange voice
On this night of May
Po-liang speaking:
"O, my people
The flame is burning
The fire
Is burning
The sacred flame
Is burning
And is always ours.
Let us go with these flames
Let us quench the enemy's flames
Here in my village—
Here where my child—

Her eyesockets
Are wide open
She stares at
The soft wind and the sand
Her sword is lifted
Her sleeves are tucked in at the elbows
She cries
She laughs
"I too must kill a man."
And in her voice
Swords, stars, blood, madness
Are crying

She cries,
But do not say she is mad.
She is China.
The woods and the forests
The rivers and the streams
Do not say she is mad.
Others are mad.
Do not say she is dead.
When there are men to kill
She never dies.

The sword never dies
China never dies . . .
>*Translated by Chu Chun-I.*

APPENDIX

THE DRUMMER OF THE AGE

By WEN YI-TUO

THE *drum is the ancestor and the king of all musical instruments, and since music cannot exist without rhythm, it cannot be independent of the use of the drum. And the drum is the source and life of music. Many epithets describe the sound of the drum: grave, stern, strong, firm, rough, excited, mysterious, but essentially the drum is male and includes the ancient male mysteries. It is the music for the beginning of life and the beginning of breath; and there can be no life without the emotions that come from the drum.*

Historically, the development of poetry and poetic music have been along the same lines. First there were percussion instruments; these were followed by instruments of pipes and strings, and the development from pure rhythm to melody followed the changes introduced by the change of instruments, in exactly the same way that the poetry of five and seven words to a line followed the poetry of three or four words to a line.[1] *In these vaster lines we see for the first time the development of melody in poetry. But it is necessary to note here that with the introduction of complex instruments and complex lines, we are presented with the spectacle of continually decreasing* emotion, *and there has grown up in time a preference for the emotion which derives from pipes and strings and even a disgust for the emotion which derives from drums.*

Why should this be so? Why should the more delicate and feeble emotions (which herald ennui *and seem to carry death within them) have precedence over the more robust and healthy emotions? At the beginning of the history of poetry in China there were simple tunes sung*

---

[1] Refers to the introduction of the five word lines in Chinese poetry by Su Wu and Li Ling of the second and first centuries B.C., who were captured by the Huns and introduced the lines from the Barbarians. In 150 B.C. the Emperor Wu Ti founded a school to encourage five and seven word lines.

to the beat of the drum. The complex instruments, the complex sounds, the "decayed music" was introduced from abroad with all its half-notes, its fashionable and unhealthy beauty. Is this the fate of poetry throughout history? Perhaps. But which is the music which heralds the new life coming to China? The music of the flute and the lute (even the lute without strings) has certainly nothing in common with our iron struggles which lead to death and blood. And so it happens that even our most modern, our most aristocratic poets have taken to the drum. Of course, they have not all succeeded perfectly in using this instrument, and many of them still utter strange, inchoate, wet, mouldy sounds, which are smeared over the sacrifices made in this war.

Therefore, when you suddenly hear a new poet proclaiming with the sounds of a drum, you cannot keep silent:

> *"One more gun!*
> *One more bullet to put the enemy to death . . ."*
>
> *Can't you hear it?*
> *Ha, it is good talk!*
>
> *Can't you hear it?*
> *We*
> *Must speedily encourage our hearts*
> *Going to battle!*
>
> *We want the fields*
> *To spring up with wheat!*
>
> *We want the fields*
> *To spring up with rice!*
>
> *Use these things:*
> > *Let them be weapons*
> > *To fight with to the end.*

(More
More.)

More grain,
More victories!
                              Tien Chien: More.

Here there are "no sound of lutes", no half-notes, no delicate arpeggios: each sentence is simple, powerful, deadly serious. These short steady sentences move with the sound of drums: they penetrate into the ears and beat with your heart-beats. You may say that it is not poetry, but if you do, it is because your ears are habituated to lute-strings and have become too delicate:

You see
Their
Vengeful
Power,
Their
Vengeful
Blood,
Their
Vengeful
Songs.
Fists are clasped!

Fists are clasped!
They want
To branch out
In thousands,
Loudly,
——Together.

> *Many thousands!*
> *Da! Da!*
> *——Together.*
>
> *Twining,*
> *Dancing . . .*
>
> *Projecting*
> *Bones,*
> *Gutted*
> *Flesh*
> *Carries the weight*
> *Of the Nation's*
> *Madness*
> *And the nation's*
> *Roaring!*
> —*Tien Chien: The People's Dance.*

Here, there is not only the music of the drum but also the emotion of the drum; the same sound which was heard when Chieh Chang of the Ching Kingdom plucked the staff from his commander when his own hand was bleeding, and the same sound which you will hear in Eugene O'Neill's "Emperor Jones", the mad African drum crackling with heat and the energy of life.

That poems such as these should be written is the first condition of poetry which pretends to have any connection with our present desire to live, our positive, absolute, desire to live. All traditional methods of versification are dismissed: here there are no comforts, no mediators, no poisons. This is not the harmful enervating music of the past. This is the sound of drums, encouraging you to love, to hate, to live with the highest degree of heat and energy. Let us therefore respect the "drummers of the age", for we have already too many delicate lute-players.

Translated by Chu Chun-I.

For Product Safety Concerns and Information please contact our EU
representative GPSR@taylorandfrancis.com
Taylor & Francis Verlag GmbH, Kaufingerstraße 24, 80331 München, Germany

www.ingramcontent.com/pod-product-compliance
Lightning Source LLC
Chambersburg PA
CBHW070618300426
44113CB00010B/1576